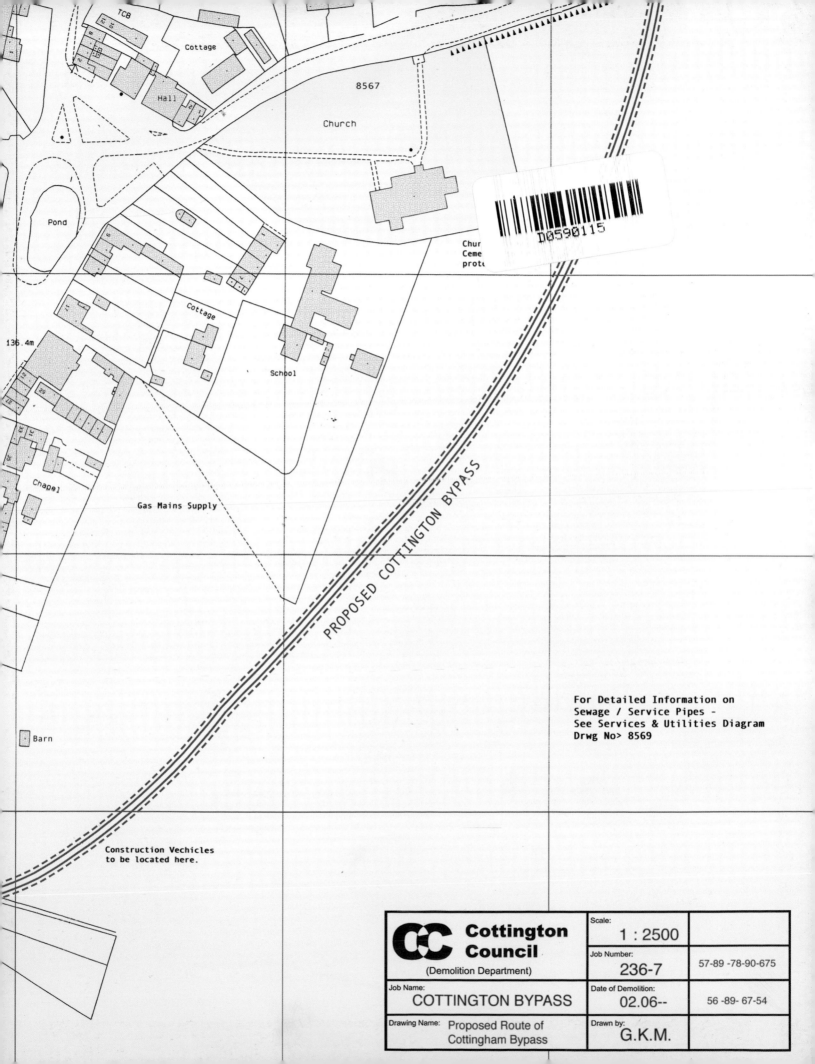

TCB

Cottage

Hall

8567

Church

Pond

Chur
Ceme
prot

136.4m

Cottage

School

Chapel

Gas Mains Supply

PROPOSED COTTINGTON BYPASS

For Detailed Information on
Sewage / Service Pipes -
See Services & Utilities Diagram
Drwg No> 8569

Barn

Construction Vechicles
to be located here.

D0590115

CC Cottington Council (Demolition Department)	Scale: **1 : 2500**	
	Job Number: **236-7**	57-89 -78-90-675
Job Name: **COTTINGTON BYPASS**	Date of Demolition: **02.06--**	56 -89- 67-54
Drawing Name: Proposed Route of Cottingham Bypass	Drawn by: **G.K.M.**	

The making of
THE HITCHHIKER'S
GUIDE TO THE GALAXY

The filming of the Douglas Adams classic

Acknowledgements

Stills photography: Laurie Sparham
Jim Henson Creature Shop photography: Tim Jetis,
Jamie Courtier, Leo Burton and Julian Manning
Second unit photography: Dominic Leung
Page 49 bottom right: © Mary Evans Picture Library
All quotations from *The Hitchhiker's Guide to the Galaxy* by
Douglas Adams reproduced by permission of Pan Macmillan

Robbie would like to thank all who gave so freely of their time for
the interviews; also Ed Victor and Grainne Fox; Natalie Jerome
who worked to make this happen on a deadline which was only
just short of impossible; Dan Newman and Paul Simpson for
elegance and words; Sue, Sam and Olivia (as always and with
love); but in this instance above everybody else, Douglas.

Paul would like to thank Tracy Morgan and Peter Mole for
stepping into the breach at the last minute, and to Alison
Sixseptante and Karen Lonsdale for other assistance.

For their help in sourcing images thanks to Lita Blechman,
Joel Collins, Anita Dhillon, Andy Fowler and Sean Mathieson

© 2005 Touchstone Pictures

First published 2005 by Boxtree
an imprint of Pan Macmillan Ltd
Pan Macmillan, 20 New Wharf Road, London N1 9RR
Basingstoke and Oxford
Associated companies throughout the world
www.panmacmillan.com

ISBN 0 752225855

Edited by Robbie Stamp, text by Paul Simpson

All photographs appear courtesy of Disney, unless otherwise specified

The right of Robbie Stamp to be identified as the
author of this work has been asserted by him in accordance
with the Copyright, Designs and Patents Act 1988.

9 8 7 6 5 4 3 2 1

A CIP catalogue record for this book is available from
the British Library.

Design by Perfect Bound Ltd
Colour Reproduction by Aylesbury Studios (Bromley) Ltd
Printed by Butler and Tanner

TOUCHSTONE PICTURES AND SPYGLASS ENTERTAINMENT PRESENT A BARBER/BIRNBAUM PRODUCTION A HAMMER AND TONGS PRODUCTION AN EVERYMAN PICTURES PRODUCTION "THE HITCHHIKER'S GUIDE TO THE GALAXY" SAM ROCKWELL MOS DEF ZOOEY DESCHANEL MARTIN FREEMAN BILL NIGHY ANNA CHANCELLOR AND JOHN MALKOVICH PRODUCERS TODD ARNOW CAROLINE HEWITT MUSIC BY JOBY TALBOT COSTUME DESIGNER SAMMY SHELDON EDITOR NIVEN HOWIE PRODUCTION DESIGNER JOEL COLLINS DIRECTOR OF PHOTOGRAPHY IGOR JADUE-LILLO EXECUTIVE PRODUCERS DOUGLAS ADAMS ROBBIE STAMP DEREK EVANS PRODUCED BY GARY BARBER ROGER BIRNBAUM NICK GOLDSMITH JAY ROACH JONATHAN GLICKMAN BASED ON THE BOOK BY DOUGLAS ADAMS SCREENPLAY BY DOUGLAS ADAMS AND KAREY KIRKPATRICK DIRECTED BY GARTH JENNINGS Distributed by BUENA VISTA PICTURES DISTRIBUTION ©TOUCHSTONE PICTURES

DON'T PANIC.

hitchhikersmovie.com

THE MAKING OF
THE HITCHHIKER'S GUIDE TO THE GALAXY

THE FILMING OF THE DOUGLAS ADAMS CLASSIC

EDITED BY ROBBIE STAMP

BOXTREE

Contents

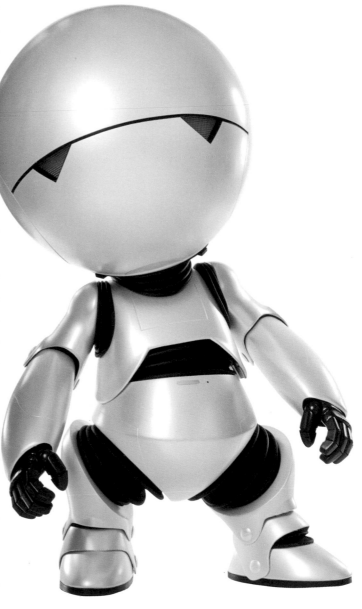

> '**It is an important and popular fact that things are not always what they seem.**'
>
> The Guide, *The Hitchhiker's Guide to the Galaxy*

Introduction

> '**I am very confident that [the film] will actually go into production any decade now. When? I want to know when, too.**'
>
> Douglas Adams, July 1995

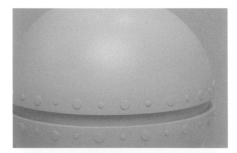

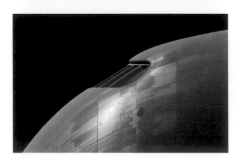

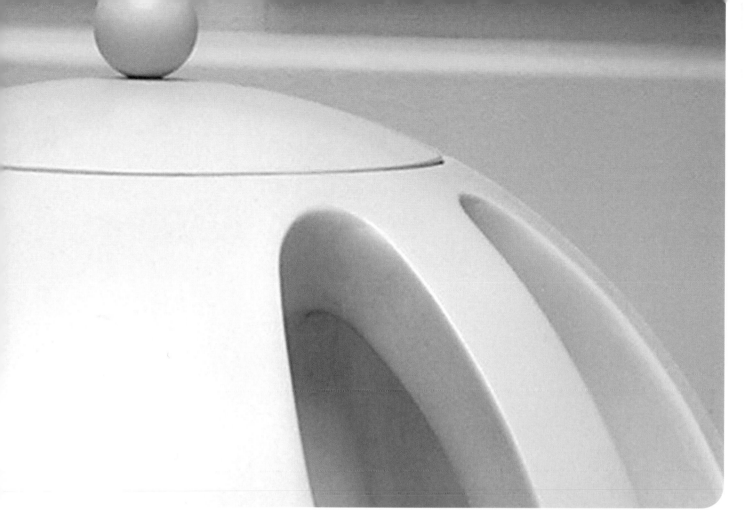

Tea, teacups and teapots play a central role in the design and construction of the *Heart of Gold* and its unique propulsion system, the Infinite Improbability Drive

In April 2005, almost ten years since Douglas Adams made that prophecy, a movie of *The Hitchhiker's Guide to the Galaxy* **opened in cinemas.**

For the first time on the big screen, audiences worldwide were able to witness the adventures of the last surviving human, Arthur Dent, as he roams the universe in the spaceship The Heart of Gold. His travelling companions include his friend Ford Prefect, who rather disconcertingly has turned out to be from a small planet in the vicinity of Betelgeuse and not from Guildford after all, the President of the Galaxy, Zaphod Beeblebrox, and Tricia Macmillan, a charming young lady who Arthur failed to hit it off with at a party in Islington shortly before the destruction of the Earth. They are also accompanied by Marvin, a manically depressed robot with a brain the size of a planet.

The Hitchhiker's Guide to the Galaxy sprang from the mind of writer Douglas Adams. He often claimed he had the original idea while hitchhiking around Europe in 1971, but it was a full seven years before The Guide's first incarnation, in a six-part radio series on BBC Radio 4. Co-written in part with producer John Lloyd, the show was an instant hit, and Douglas was commissioned by Pan to write a book based on the series.

That first book went straight to the top of the best-sellers' list, selling a quarter of a million copies in three months. A stage version, presented by Ken Campbell, was a success. A 'Christmas Special' radio episode was soon followed by a further five instalments. Two LPs, one a recording of the first four episodes, the second of the next two, were released. The Guide made the transition to television, in a six-part version produced by Alan J. W. Bell. Douglas reworked material from the final eight episodes of the radio series into a second book, *The Restaurant at the End of the Universe*.

'Apathetic bloody planet,
I've no sympathy at all.'

Prostetnic Vogon Jeltz, *The Hitchhiker's Guide to the Galaxy*

Reproduced with kind permission of Pan Macmillan

'The problem with turning Hitchhikers into a feature was that it wasn't always developed with the story as its central driving force. It's driven by ideas.'

Screenwriter Karey Kirkpatrick

The only mainstream format in which the tale had not been told was the cinema. But it took from 1979 to 2005 to make that a reality.

After completing work on the third Hitchhikers novel, *Life, the Universe and Everything* (adapted from a proposed screenplay for a *Doctor Who* movie), Douglas spent a year in Los Angeles working with *Ghostbusters* director Ivan Reitman on a prospective screenplay, but that came to nothing.

Having repeatedly said that he would not write another Hitchhikers book, Douglas returned to the UK and wrote *So Long and Thanks for All the Fish* before becoming involved with the Hitchhikers computer game from Infocom, which once again revisited the destruction of the Earth and Arthur Dent's arrival on board the Heart of Gold. Douglas would return to the Hitchhikers universe one final time in novel form, with the publication of *Mostly Harmless* in 1992.

That same year, after buying back the movie rights from Columbia Pictures, Douglas met Michael Nesmith, formerly of The Monkees pop group, now a TV and film producer, and worked with him trying to get the movie made. This too unfortunately failed to attract the necessary Hollywood backing.

However, when *Men in Black* did extraordinarily well at cinemas in 1997, comedy and science fiction became a more attractive combination in Hollywood. Douglas and his friend and business partner, Robbie Stamp, were introduced to Roger Birnbaum at the independent production company Caravan Pictures which had the muscle and enthusiasm to bring Disney on board, and *Austin Powers* director Jay Roach, who also had a strong relationship with Disney. Douglas and Jay struck up a strong creative relationship almost immediately.

FOR SCALE APPROVAL

Jeltz/Kwalz   Councilor   Soldier   Minion

Above: Garth loves testing props
Far left: The Vogon height chart showing Garth, Nick and Nick's dog Mack to scale
Near left: Executive producer Robbie Stamp looks through the lens

Assorted problems still beset the project, and at the time of Douglas Adams' sudden death in May 2001, neither the creative nor logistical difficulties of a *Hitchhiker's Guide to the Galaxy* movie had been solved. However, with the blessing of Douglas's widow, Jane Belson, Robbie Stamp worked with Roger Birnbaum (who by then had formed a new company with new partner Gary Barber, called Spyglass Entertainment) to keep the project moving. Through Jay Roach, the screenwriter Karey Kirkpatrick came on board, and he worked from the most recent revision to the script that Douglas had worked on, as well as earlier versions retrieved from Douglas's hard drives.

'The problem with turning Hitchhikers into a feature was that it wasn't always developed with the story as its central driving force,' Kirkpatrick explains. 'It's driven by ideas. Douglas is brilliant at the editorializing, the social satire and the incredible conceptual stuff. The trick was to arrange that

into an accessible story, which I hope we did.'

When Jay Roach had to step down from directing the film because of other movie commitments, he remained on board as a producer and sent the script to fellow director Spike Jonze, but he was unavailable, and instead suggested working with the British partnership of Hammer and Tongs, aka director Garth Jennings and producer Nick Goldsmith.

'None of it was conventional,' Garth says. 'Everything was conceptually so different from anything else you would ever have seen. We're quite good at that side of things. It also needed something that you had a strong feeling for. Every single idea in that script is so wonderful and funny, and has a depth to it. I always felt that our silliest, stupidest stuff, whether it was something involving a person or a creature, would always have a heart and soul to it. It was a chance for us to apply all the things that we enjoy doing to telling a story on a big scale, with even more heart and soul.'

Above: The pre-production art department produced many hundreds of concepts for every aspect of the film. These concepts were often reworked repeatedly by different artists
Far left: Production Designer Joel Collins with Nick and Garth

Working with their regular production designer, Joel Collins, Nick and Garth conceived the incredible visuals at the heart of *The Hitchhiker's Guide to the Galaxy*. They filled a room at propmakers Asylum with drawings and ideas for every lifeform, planet and spaceship that would populate the universe. 'They gave us their gymnasium,' Garth remembers, 'and I reckon we had about two thousand drawings on the walls at one point. It was a massive room and you couldn't see the walls for drawings.'

'We had to understand how it would look, so we could tell Disney, Spyglass, Robbie and everyone else exactly what Nick and Garth's vision for the universe was going to be,' Joel adds. The aim was to create a universe which they could bring to life in the studio, rather than wait to achieve everything in post-production. It was their enthusiasm and ethos that eventually persuaded Disney to give the project a green light. And on 19 April 2004, first assistant director Richard Whelan called 'action' on the first shot of *The Hitchhiker's Guide to the Galaxy*.

'Getting to that moment was nigh-on a 25-year saga,' Robbie Stamp recalls. 'It was a great moment and it did bring a tear to my eye. I was proud that we'd got to that point, but so sad that Douglas wasn't there to share it.'

Setting the scene

Much has changed in the world of screen science fiction during the quarter of a century that the movie of *The Hitchhiker's Guide to the Galaxy* has been in development. The arrival of *Star Wars™* in 1977 had various repercussions. Science fiction was popular once more, with advances in model technology allowing more realistic scenes than ever before. When Hitchhikers' first screen incarnation appeared

Deep Thought was not computer-generated for the film; he was a large model (**above left**). Computers added the crowds wating for The Answer – see page 102

in 1981, it was state of the art British TV SF. Yet in America a worrying trend had begun, with special effects dominating shows such as *Battlestar Galactica*.

The advent of computer graphics in the 1982 spin-off film *Star Trek II: The Wrath of Khan* was hailed as a saviour by many in the industry, with movies such as *Terminator 2: Judgement Day*, and later *The Matrix* trilogy spending millions of dollars on major effects sequences. It almost reached a point where characters seemed to be irrelevant, as long as they could be seen doing six impossible things before breakfast. The new *Star Wars™* trilogy was accused of sacrificing plot and characterization in favour of glittering computer graphics sequences, while even the James Bond franchise finally accepted the inevitable and incorporated computer-generated effects into 2002's *Die Another Day*.

A backlash was inevitable. While there is no denying that computer effects nowadays are incredibly realistic, they somehow lack the immediacy of performance that comes from an effect or creature in the studio. Actors tend to react better to a large head looming in their eyeline than to a balloon on a stick which will be replaced by the computer with something terrifying. And when directors view a rough assembly of footage, it's clear exactly what is going on because it actually happened in the studio.

Like any item in a director's arsenal, computer graphics are a tool to be used, in the same way as cinema pioneer Georges Méliès learned what could be done with the simple expedient of stopping the camera, rearranging the scene, and restarting, giving an apparently seamless, instantaneous change. *The Hitchhiker's Guide to the Galaxy* called on every single tool in Garth Jennings' arsenal ...

The last ever dolphin message was misinterpreted as a surprisingly sophisticated attempt to do a double-backward somersault through a hoop while whistling The Star-Spangled Banner, but in fact the message was this...

'So long and thanks for all the fish.'

The Guide, *The Hitchhiker's Guide to the Galaxy*

The dolphins at play
at Lauro Park

Earth

The Opening Titles

'Garth and I have always loved big title sequences,' producer Nick Goldsmith says. 'Titles which have meaning, not just words on a page. The idea was to pull the viewers into the film quickly, and give them an idea of what they were about to expect.'

'We were trying to make this film different from the start,' director Garth Jennings adds. 'We wanted to grab everyone. We're all big fans of *Singing in the Rain* and those old movies that sat you down, got you comfortable, tucked you in, opened everything up and did a really good job of clearing the decks.'

Nick and Garth decided to start the movie with a big production number. 'We have to do an awful lot in that opening two minutes,' Garth continues. 'Set the film up, set the language up, and appease the fans of the original. We're telling them, "Don't worry – it's in good hands. It's going to be bigger and different, but in the spirit of the original material." The music really helps you do that.'

SWIMMING WITH DOLPHINS

The dolphins were very quick to make their displeasure felt if they didn't like what the Second Unit were doing in their home. 'On the third day of filming at the dolphinarium, they were setting up to do the underwater bits, and had a cameraman under the water,' Nick Goldsmith says. 'Dom (Second Unit director Dominic Leung) wanted to be able to communicate with the cameraman so they put in a loudspeaker system under the water, and it freaked the dolphins out so much that only one came out. Fair enough: there was some funny man in the water.'

'We definitely ruined that afternoon's show,' Dominic Leung says ruefully. 'We were trying to cause as little disturbance as possible, but that was our fault. The optimum number for a show was six dolphins, so one wasn't really enough.'

'It's brilliant when all the ideas start clicking.'
Director Garth Jennings

Composer Joby Talbot worked with Nick and Garth on an opening song in the style of those old 1950s' musicals. 'With that style of music, you've got more licence,' Garth explains. 'Everyone enjoys this music, and knows it's about being fun and uplifting and innocent.'

Garth describes the process of creating the title sequence as 'one of the easiest things in the world to do. We turned up at Joby's house and within six or seven hours we had the piece. It's brilliant when all the ideas start clicking.'

The original plan was to start the titles with some home video footage shot by Nick and Garth at SeaWorld in San Diego, and then segue into library footage of dolphins. 'We cut together the song with all stock stuff, but realized that we weren't going to find everything that would give the effect we needed,' Nick recalls. 'We started looking for dolphinariums that would be friendly for us to film in, and ended up finding Lauro Park in Tenerife, which is also a parrot sanctuary. Garth and I were filming by then, so our Second Unit went out. They were good, and incredibly helpful there. They cared about their dolphins, and they made it clear that we had to work around them, and their dolphins, not the other way around.'

'They didn't normally do night shoots, but we coaxed them into doing a few shots at night,' Second Unit director Dominic Leung says. 'We got some lights sent over especially for the shot where the dolphins leap up in the moonlight and don't come back down again. The staff were really helpful all through the shoot.'

Before writing the title song, composer Joby Talbot researched the period musicals that Garth wanted to emulate. 'I watched lots of Busby Berkeley movies,' he says. 'They were so brilliantly done. It's just gag after gag after gag, the way they choreograph is so clever, and the orchestrations are just great. Our original idea was to take our song much further, and have a waltz section and a high kick section, but in the event it's a much more straight-down-the-line three- part song. All we knew was it was called 'So Long and Thanks For All the Fish', and I just had this tune in my mind from the rhythm of the words.'

Joby spent an evening with the film's orchestrator Chris Austin composing the verse. 'We decided the essence of writing a really good piece of this kind of music, which is so consummately professional, is that it should have the most beautiful chords possible,' Joby explains. 'If you were to play them in a very slow way or arrange them for a string orchestra, they would be as heartrending as Samuel Barber's *Adagio for Strings*, but play them fast and they sound all pizzazzy. Once I got two verses together, I invited Garth to dinner. He was very encouraging – by halfway through the verse he was laughing and jumping around the room and loved it. He grabbed a pen and paper, and started scribbling down ideas for lyrics. A few weeks later, we all got together, wrote the lyrics, and I then tidied it up to give it a bit more shape.'

Opposite: 2nd Unit director Dominic Leung and 2nd AD David Cain
Below: The 2nd unit crew and dolphin trainers

Arthur's house

Arthur Dent is not happy on this Thursday morning. He is regretting a missed opportunity at a party he recently attended, and someone wants to knock his house down to build a by-pass. To cap it all, his friend Ford Prefect insists on taking him to the pub because he has some important news for him ...

'Arthur's house comes straight out of the book,' Garth says. 'Our location manager drove around Hertfordshire for two days, and pulled up at the side of the road where he could see this farmhouse. Not only visually was it what I wanted in terms of being ordinary and having fields around it, but 500 yards up the road, it had a farm area with the perfect space for a unit base where you could turn trucks round. There was also a space which was remarkably similar to the house in the book with nothing on it, where they were perfectly happy for us to build Arthur's destroyed house.'

Although the scenes at Arthur's home are the first to be seen in the film, they weren't the first to be shot. Scenes for movies are filmed out of order, and then assembled in the editing room. All the scenes in one location, whether it's an exterior like Arthur's house in Hertfordshire, or an interior

set such as the Heart of Gold at Elstree Studios, are normally filmed together, no matter where they appear in the finished product. 'It was nice to get outside after filming on the Heart of Gold,' Nick Goldsmith recalls. 'We were lucky, and we had good weather while we were there.'

Set decorator Kate Beckly was pleased with the choice of location, as it minimized the amount of work that was required. 'Amazingly a lot of the dressing that Joel and I had discussed was already there in the house!' she explains. 'There was stripy wallpaper in his bedroom, which gave the feeling that Arthur was in a kind of cage. The vibe of the house was pretty much as we wanted it, and it just needed to become the home of a thirty-year-old man, rather than an elderly couple.'

Production designer Joel Collins worked with Beckly and graphics designer Anita Dhillon to create a complete existence for Arthur. Every aspect of his life was specifically designed and fabricated, from his council tax bills to a letter about his library fines. 'Joel and I talked about what sorts of things Arthur was keen on,' Beckley recalls. 'There were minute discussions about the sorts of things he'd read. When Martin Freeman came onto the set, he was amazed at the detailed level of dressing. We even had the copy of the *Radio Times* marked up with all the programmes that he wanted to watch that week.'

Left: Ford Prefect goes to greet Earth's dominant lifeform
Below left: The pub's customers prepare for The End
Below right: Ford encourages Arthur to drink up

For Mos Def, Ford's entrance to the film set the tone for the character. 'He arrives on a shopping cart full of beer and peanuts coming down a hill towards the bulldozers that Arthur's laying in front of,' he says. 'It really made me feel that Ford was going to be this very way-out sort of guy because when you see him on Earth, he does look off-his-trolley! There's a very sort of matter-of-fact thing about him that makes him seem even more daft. I love that sense of precision to him and doing physical things, especially on this film, as it has required a certain physical sharpness from all of us.'

The pub to which Ford drags Arthur was very close to the house location. 'It was a functional drinking pub,' Beckley adds. 'It was almost perfect as it was.' The proximity of the pub was particularly useful, as it allowed the unit to shoot the scene there at short notice if weather conditions meant that outside filming at Arthur's house was impossible.

In the pub, Arthur regales Ford with the tale of his encounter with Tricia. The party at which they met was in fact the very first scene that was shot for the movie, on 19 April 2004. One of co-producer Todd Arnow's responsibilities was to create a shooting schedule that included all the requirements of the production. 'There was talk early on about shooting on the Heart of Gold set first,' he explains, 'but the majority of those scenes involve all four of our main ensemble actors, and I felt that Garth would probably be best off starting the movie focussing on getting performances out of two actors rather than four. We felt it would be a nice way to start filming the movie with something of an intimate, almost introductory scene between Zooey and Martin, and help them build into their characters. It was a fun scene, with background extras, and I thought Garth would feel very comfortable directing it.'

In addition to the months of pre-production, during which Garth, Nick and their team had been preparing everything that was needed for the film, there had also been two weeks of rehearsals with the actors. Garth remembers that on the night before shooting commenced, 'it felt like we were incredibly prepared. This film was an exam and we'd been revising like crazy. I really enjoyed shooting the party, and I knew at the end of the first day that anything we did the next day would just be a bonus.'

Producer Nick Goldsmith wasn't overawed by shooting on the first day of his feature debut. 'If you've done your job right, everything is worked out well before the first day,' he points out. 'I was excited standing there when they were going to say "turn over", but I remember it not being as exciting as I thought it was going to be.'

Arthur's unhappy memories of the party are interrupted by the start of demolition work on his house. To achieve this, a duplicate of Arthur's house was built up the road from the farmhouse by construction co-ordinator Steve Bohan and his team. 'We built the house in sections,' Steve recalls. 'Special effects rigged it so that they could fall away when the bulldozers were hitting it. Any stuff we knew was going to stay on the ground was made from plaster, but the other sections were fibreglass so that they could be stood back up again.'

'The false house was quite a tough build,' Kate Beckly adds. 'When we needed sunshine, it was raining, and when we needed rain it was sunny. We had the most dreadful rain all through the build – the plasterers were out there in the pouring rain trying to dry the plaster, and the painters were trying to do their job. Eventually it all came good, but it was a photo finish! Joel had an incredible attention to detail, and kept requiring more wire or roof joists. It was not as simple as you'd imagine to build a demolished house from scratch!

'It must have been a massive headache for the location manager getting all those huge construction vehicles up that tiny single-track lane,' she continues. 'It was complete mayhem. After the twentieth JCB went past, the location manager turned to me and asked if there were any more, and I told him there were another five to come!'

BLINK AND YOU'LL MISS...

Throughout the film Kate Beckly and Anita Dhillon added little touches to the production that reflect elements of Douglas Adams' life and writings. The village of Cottington, where Arthur lives, is where Douglas was born. At the party, Arthur is reading *The Selfish Gene*, by Douglas's friend Richard Dawkins. And the number 42 (the Ultimate Answer to Life, the Universe and Everything) turns up in numerous places – on vehicle number plates, for instance – and there's a postcard of New York's 42nd Street on the bookcase at the party where Arthur meets Trillian.

Opposite top: The model shoot and artwork for Arthur's destroyed house
Opposite middle: Ford interrupts Prosser's attempt to drive a bulldozer through Arthur's house
Opposite bottom: Early visuals for the party and guests

IS THIS GUY BORING YOU?

The party was shot on a two-tier set at Elstree and, for some of the cast and crew, it really did feel as if they were on a rooftop. It's the first time that the meeting between Arthur and Tricia MacMillan has ever been seen on film, and a lot of thought went into the details. 'We knew it was going to be a fancy dress party,' Executive producer Robbie Stamp notes. 'We had worked out the jokes. We wanted Tricia to go dressed as Charles Darwin, because we liked the idea of a beautiful woman in a snowy white beard (above), and also it would be an in-joke. Anybody who knew Douglas knew that he loved to read everything he could get his hands on about evolution, it was one of the great passions of his life. It was enormous fun, and later on when Arthur and Trillian moved to the rooftop, we filmed that iconic entrance for Zaphod.'

The Cast

'Early on, we assembled our ideal cast, then the process went right around the houses, as we looked at all the hot young things for the roles, and we came back to the people who were perfect for it,' Garth Jennings says bluntly. 'The cast all worked really well together, and they're really sweet and funny. We logged onto websites and started pulling down pictures to assemble on the desktop to see how they looked together.'

It was important that there wasn't a single 'star' to the film – Hitchhikers has always been an ensemble story. 'I felt that if we went for a big star for Zaphod, for example, it would unbalance the film,' Robbie Stamp says. 'It would turn into Zaphod's movie – the star and their team would have demanded more and more, and the gravitational pull would have shifted in the wrong direction. We needed people who liked the idea of being part of a good ensemble cast.'

Arthur Dent (Martin Freeman)

'We knew we wanted to expand on the human story,' Garth recalls, 'and we're fans of films like *The Apartment*. We thought that Arthur was like the young Jack Lemmon in that film: slightly stuck in his ways, hypochondriac, neurotic, someone who can be really stupid and irritating and yet completely sympathetic. Martin Freeman was one of our first thoughts for the role.'

Hitchhiker tradition has it that Arthur Dent travels the universe in his dressing gown, and Martin Freeman was resigned to being stuck in one throughout the shoot. 'I didn't mind as long as it didn't look like a joke and we were judging him before he even opened his mouth,' he says. 'As long as he looked like a normal person who lived in the normal world, that was all I needed to know because then I could play him as a normal person.'

'I don't feel well. I need a cup of tea.'

Arthur Dent, *The Hitchhiker's Guide to the Galaxy*

Ironically, for the character who was dressed more like an everyday human than anyone else in the film, Arthur's costumes proved the most difficult to find the fabric for. 'I wanted to make a dressing gown that was slightly over-big, and just slightly tweaked,' costume designer Sammy Sheldon explains. 'We wanted it to be made from towelling, and we had to wait five weeks for the right material to come from the Czech Republic. We couldn't buy decent pyjama striped fabric that didn't have blue or green in it – because of the special effects, we couldn't have either of those colours. We had fabric sent over from Turkey, and tried printing it, but it went disastrously wrong. We even had problems with his safari suit for the party because the company that made them had decided to stop, and we finally found a roll of the right fabric in the back of someone's shop!'

Opposite: Ford tries desperately to hitch a lift over the doomed planet

'It's a tough galaxy. You want to survive out here, you really gotta know where your towel is.'

Ford Prefect, *The Hitchhiker's Guide to the Galaxy*

Opposite bottom: Ford's thumb ring

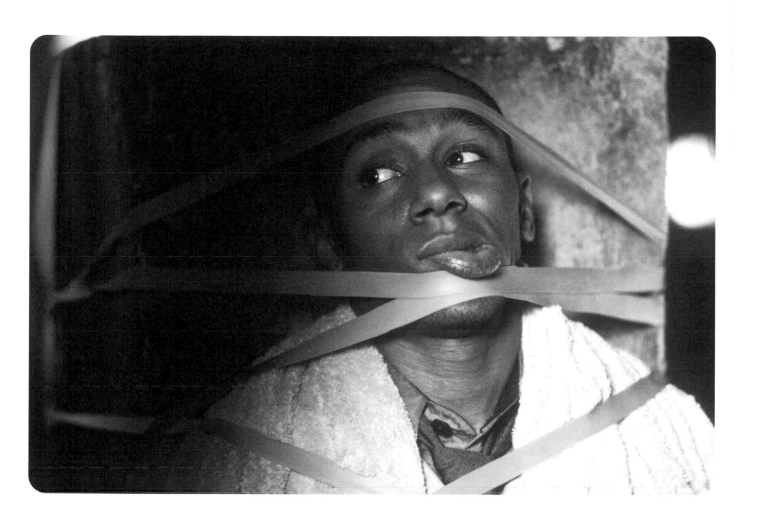

Ford Prefect (Mos Def)

Rap artist Mos Def came on board Hitchhikers at the suggestion of casting director Suzie Figgis, who had seen him perform at the Royal Court Theatre. Within 20 minutes of sitting down with Nick and Garth at Soho House in New York, the producer and director were impressed by his take on the character and his philosophy. 'Ford needed to have an ineffable cool about him,' Robbie Stamp notes, 'with that Zen-like quality you'd have if you were a researcher for *The Hitchhiker's Guide to the Galaxy*. Who would you most like to have beside you in a sticky situation? Someone who's negotiated his way through many different planetary cultures. Mos was really smart, and when amongst the other actors, he gave the ensemble cast a really interesting dynamic.'

After some debate about whether Ford would be dressed in alien or human clothing, Sammy Sheldon elected to go for 'something very classical, a three-piece suit that he looks slightly bizarre in. Mos is a stylish guy and knows what suits him. His hat came from an army store, and we put some purple inside it. The underneaths of all his collars are purple – all the colours are sneaking out.'

'I want to go
somewhere
I've never
been, and I
want to go
with you.'

Trillian, *The Hitchhiker's
Guide to the Galaxy*

Trillian [Tricia MacMillan] (Zooey Deschanel)

Casting Trillian, Garth was very keen to avoid the modern kick-ass type of heroine, someone who would be able to kung fu her way through space. Nor did he want her to be simply a brainy astrophysicist, although it was clear from the script that she was highly intelligent. 'What I think Garth saw in Zooey was "the weird girl",' Executive producer Robbie Stamp comments. 'She was a bit unusual, a bit different and she had an edge to her. It was there in the very first screen test that she did with Martin.'

'Garth wanted her to look utilitarian, rather than being the "sex chick in space",' Sammy Sheldon says. 'Zooey looks great in this jump-suit. We had seven of them altogether for all the different scenes. Her reading glasses are a 1950s pair – we tried to make everything look like it came from loads of different places.'

Trillian's half-human nature is one of the few major alterations to the Hitchhikers' myth. 'The story is all about Arthur,' Robbie explains, 'and we wanted to drive the point home that he really was the last surviving human. We felt that that was emotionally worth more than slavishly following the book.'

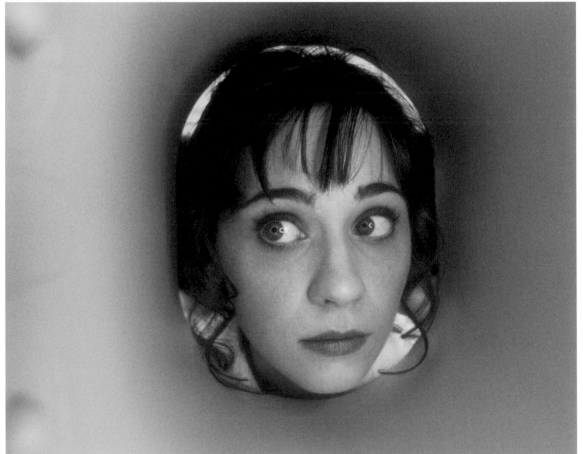

Top left: Trillian sends Marvin to pick up the hitchhikers
Top right: Enjoying Arthur's welcome home party
Bottom left: Demonstrating the Sensomatic machine
Bottom right: Arguing with Arthur on the surface of Viltvodle VI

Zaphod Beeblebrox (Sam Rockwell)

Although Sam Rockwell has made the part of Zaphod Beeblebrox very much his own, he originally auditioned for the part of Ford Prefect. However, as the audition process continued, it was clear that he was more interested in playing Zaphod. 'Garth really liked his energy and his commitment,' Robbie Stamp comments, 'and he's the kind of slightly edgy character actor that Garth likes. When he had his long hair and a sort of "rock god" feel, he had a terrific energy. He's got a lot of sex appeal, and Zaphod is a lot about sex.'

'We couldn't just clad him with stuff that looked ridiculous for the sake of being ridiculous,' Sammy Sheldon points out. 'He may be tasteless but at the same time he looks very sexy. I wanted his outfit to look a bit like a peacock: his coat is like a huge fantail, and there are lines to give a subliminal impression of movement. He has a Napoleonic collar while the front is taken from a political group from the 1820s called the Macaroni. They had very tight legs, and puffed-up chests. I made everything asym-metrical with the line down the side with the third arm. Sam Rockwell was brilliant at coming up with sugges-tions and helping take it all a stage further.'

'Zaphod's just this guy, you know?'

Gag Halfrunt, *The Hitchhiker's Guide to the Galaxy*

THE MAKING OF **THE HITCHHIKER'S GUIDE TO THE GALAXY**

Zaphod's sunglasses accentuated his cool. 'The more ridiculous they were, the better,' Costume Designer Sammy Sheldon says. 'We ended up with something that looked like the front of a car bumper. They had to be oversized, and he carried them off very well.'

'People of Earth, this is Prostetnic Vogon Jeltz of the Galactic Hyperspace Planning Council. As you are probably aware, plans for the development of the outlying regions of the galaxy involve the building of a hyperspace express route through your star system, and your planet is one of those scheduled for demolition.'

Prostetnic Vogon Jeltz, *The Hitchhiker's Guide to the Galaxy*

Top: The Vogon ship looms over Jodrell Bank – and the neighboroughing sheep

The End of the World

Ford has revealed that he is an alien, and has been trying to warn Arthur that the Vogons are on the way to destroy the Earth. Fortunately, he is able to use an electronic thumb to hitch a ride for them on board the Vogon ship, just as the planet is blown to pieces ...

To film humanity's desperate attempts to communicate with the Vogons, the unit moved to Jodrell Bank where many of the real scientists played themselves as extras on screen. The production was even able to persuade the scientists to divert the giant telescope from its deep space mission for a few hours.

'We decided to have an establishing shot of the telescope from a field a mile or so away,' assistant location manager Camilla Stephenson recalls, 'and I negotiated with the farmer that his sheep would be in the foreground. I was calling from the field telling them to move the telescope left or right, or up and down a degree, exactly as we needed it for the shot. The sheep then decided to go into a clump at the other end of the field, so the farmer shook a bucket of their feed, and they all stampeded back towards us like a herd of buffalo!'

Filming the chaos in London at the end of the world was also a major logistical exercise for the Second Unit. 'You know when you film something like that, you're going to cause havoc in the centre of London,' Stephenson explains. 'So we decided to film over a weekend when it's quieter. We could show the iconic things like underground signs and stations. We chose a typical street where we knew we could work with the number of extras we had, and the police assisted us with traffic control.'

THE STREETS OF LONDON

Among the extras in the London scene were many of Douglas Adams's family, including his daughter Polly, his mother, his sisters Sue and Jane and his brother James. 'We were originally going to be in the scene in the pub, but that was used for "weather cover", so they couldn't let us know when it was going to be filmed,' James says, 'so Robbie arranged for us to be in the scenes in London. We were really treated well, and it was a bittersweet feeling to be there without Douglas. We were sitting in a table outside a café when they filmed the panic when the Vogons arrive – they didn't give us any specific direction, but we soon realized why, since it was meant to be total chaos. My mother was at the next table, reading a newspaper, but she ignored all the panic, and just carried on reading as if nothing unusual was happening.'

Artwork for the
destruction of Earth
sequence

'The destruction of the Earth is one of the big shots for us, and took a lot of work to get all the factors right,' visual effects producer Andy Fowler comments.

Every scene in *The Hitchhiker's Guide to the Galaxy* was visualized by director Garth Jennings in a series of storyboards, which showed exactly what he expected to see eventually on the screen. These storyboards were a key element in creating the various big special effects sequences that punctuate the movie at regular intervals. From these, production designer Joel Collins and his team created computer animations in what's known as the pre-viz[ualization] process. 'The key work that was done by Joel and the pre-viz team provided us with the essential information that we could go off and take a stage further,' Andy explains.

'Before we started working with Cinesite, we were probably up to version 20 of the pre-viz getting the timings of this sequence right,' visual effects supervisor Angus Bickerton says. 'Garth always wanted to eschew the obvious, continual pull-back shot, and has gone for the jump-cut feel. We had to get the scale right so that the Vogon ship dominated Arthur's house.'

'When you've got an item in close-up, and there's a lot of depth to the background, something a thousand feet distant can look like it's only five feet away,' Fowler continues. 'It's a constant battle to get these ridiculously and comically enormous ships onto the screen. You end up putting a scale reference, like a Boeing 747, into the shot to make it clear.'

'There are some scale cheats involved in the pull-back,' Bickerton adds. 'The Vogon ships are 1 mile high by ¼ mile wide at the base, but when you pull back to see the whole Earth on the screen, they'd come out as pinheads over the planet. We change the scale of them as we pull back.'

The creation of the sequence was greatly helped when it could be timed alongside composer Joby Talbot's temporary score for the scene. 'We did a first version to a piece by composer James Horner,' Bickerton says, 'then we used Joby's piano track, and then his first pass at the score with the full orchestra. That was fabulous – from that we could create the definitive version.'

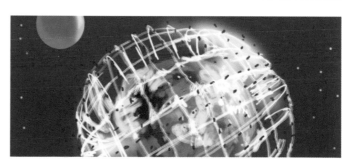
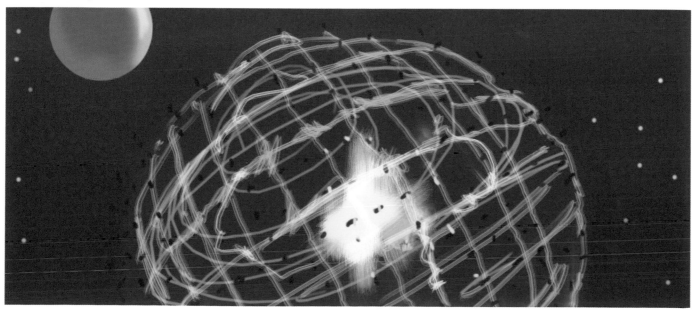

'The Hitchhiker's Guide to the Galaxy is a wholly remarkable book.'

The Guide, *The Hitchhiker's Guide to the Galaxy*

The Guide

One of the key conceptual decisions that Nick and Garth quickly made about the depiction of *The Hitchhiker's Guide to the Galaxy* was that it shouldn't be something that was absolutely the latest in technology. Nothing ages faster than yesterday's science fiction, and something that is cutting-edge now is the centrepiece of an advertisement 18 months later.

'It's not about technology, it's about hitchhiking and travel,' Garth says. 'That's why we decided to concentrate on things which were practical and durable. And that's where we came up with the idea of the Swiss Army knife – it's the perfect traveller's item. It's got everything you might need.'

It took some considerable time before Garth decided that the Swiss Army knife was conceptually what he was after, and during the pre-production period, computer graphics experts Shynola came up with numerous different ideas.

'We did a complete square version of a Swiss Army knife, but that was a little bit too much of a pastiche,' Garth notes. 'We just took the concept. It has all these grooves where the items slot in, and they suggest the pages of a book. We took the red enamel with the gold top and bottom, and joined it up one side, and that became the Guide itself.'

As far as the interior was concerned, 'we didn't want any buttons,' he notes. 'It was a touch screen, with no groovy interface that would date very quickly, just simple tabs. Shynola did the most incredible work on The Guide.'

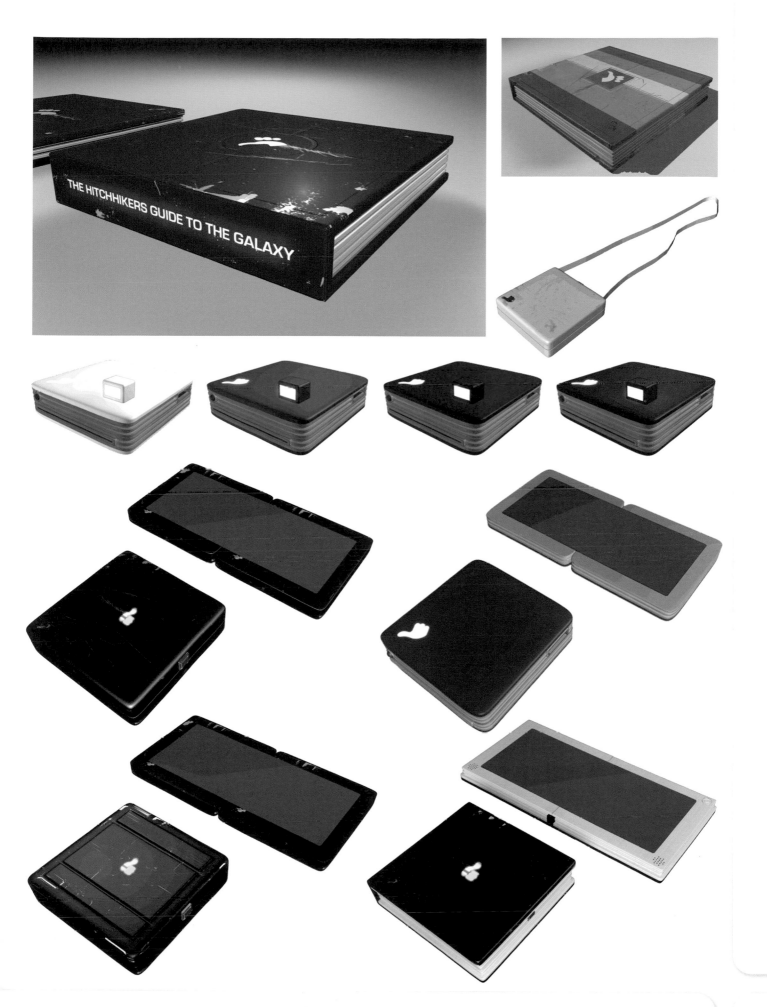

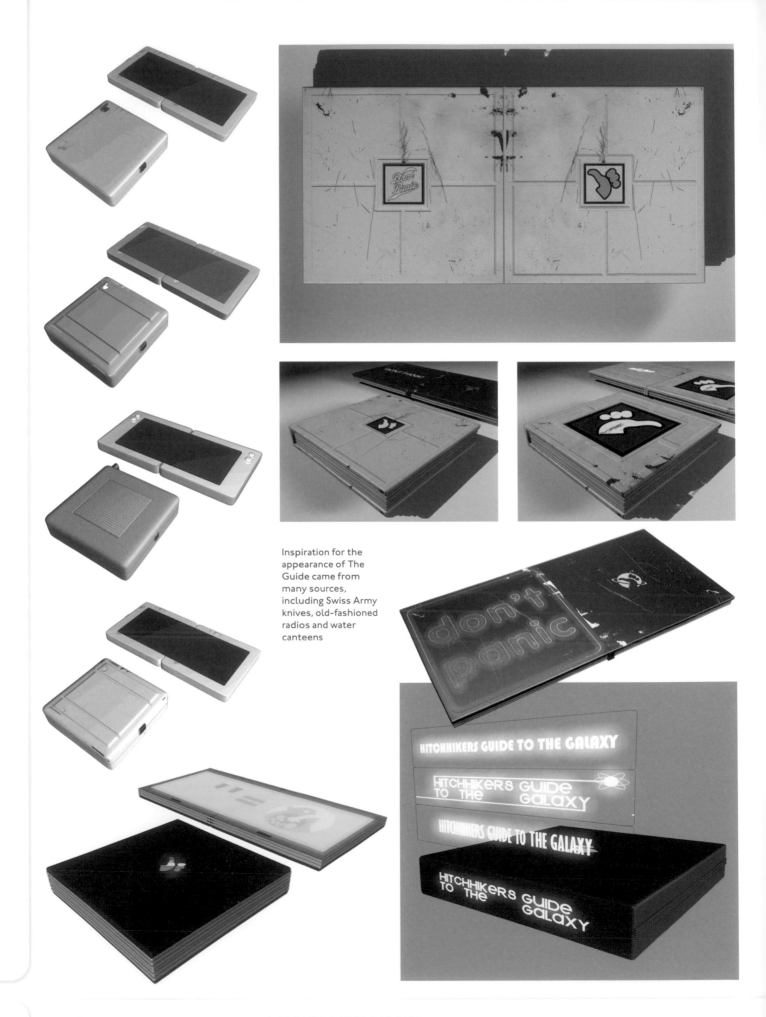

Inspiration for the appearance of The Guide came from many sources, including Swiss Army knives, old-fashioned radios and water canteens

'Garth wanted us to base the colour scheme on a rainbow so it was the most friendly and inclusive bright thing possible.'

Gideon Baws, Shynola

For The Guide entries themselves, Garth stayed with a similar approach. 'We can't compete with *The Matrix* and the way they showed information on a computer,' he points out, 'and we came back to the same point. This is something universal that has to work and be understood. We wanted simple graphic layouts, limited colour palettes for each display, and bold uses of space, so you'd have one little thing going on in one corner of the screen, then tons of space and the menu system. We reduce the elements of the entry to their basic form, and then tell stories with them.'

'Initially, we were just given the dialogue,' Shynola's Gideon Baws explains. 'We came up with multiple ways of playing out the visuals, and then presented Nick and Garth with four or five complete storyboards for each. Our initial ideas were more abstract and trying to get away from the meaning of the text, but they came back to being more functional and literal. In parallel we were working on the design, and setting up a series of rules to try to let you know that this was a real computer and it worked in a recognizable way. Garth wanted us to base the colour scheme on a rainbow so it was the most friendly and inclusive bright thing possible. We then boiled that down to one workable look.'

Using Premiere and After Effects computer programs, Shynola then moved onto the animatics stage, which look like very simple cartoons. 'They still looked like thumbnail drawings, but moved to the timings,' Gideon continues. 'Then we would do a more worked-up colour version with properly designed characters so we could see if the characters could do what we wanted them to do. Sometimes, particularly with things like the Vogons, it was very hard to get them to do pretty much anything. We had to tone down the amount they were going to do because of their physicality.'

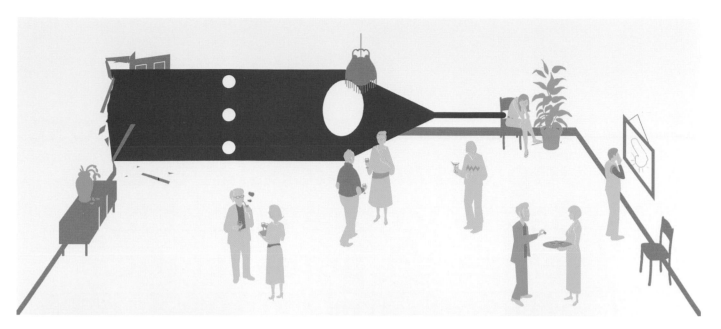

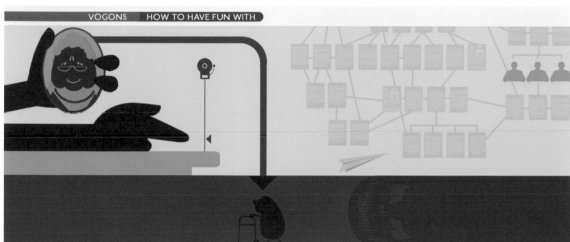

Early concepts for the Guide graphics

These animatics were then incorporated into the various edits that Niven Howie and his team prepared, and both editor and graphics designer realized that what had worked in a stand-alone form would require further changes to the timing to work as part of the edited film. 'Niven gave us back the animatics cut to the right length, and we built all the characters and the worlds, environments and backgrounds in the Maya program in three dimensions. Finally we'd make the final versions of the figures from the edited animatics, and animate them to the timings.'

The choice of actor and writer Stephen Fry as the voice of The Guide was very apposite, since he and Douglas Adams were old friends. 'We both had in common the miracle that is the Macintosh computer,' Fry recalls. 'He was delightful company, and I knew him and Jane from about 1985.'

He was delighted to be asked to play The Guide. 'I did a guide track in November 2004,' he explains. 'I knew they'd seen a lot of other people, and I was fully confident that they would get someone like Tom Hanks to do the real one!'

Fry tried to emulate the qualities displayed by Peter Jones, the original radio and television voice of the Guide. 'The key is that extraordinary mixture of authority and friendliness, which is very difficult for a lot of people to shake out of their heads,' he says. 'But of course, the largest audience of Hitchhikers in English is American and most of them don't know the radio recordings — they know the books or Douglas' own recordings on tape.'

Fry's narration is taken at a slightly slower pace than the original radio episodes. 'It has to, to go with the visuals,' Fry says. 'When the human brain has to absorb visuals and sounds, you've got to give a bit of space. With radio, you're buried in the language and nothing else.'

Fry recorded various versions of the entries 'for the various landmarks in the post production process. Sometimes I'm doing it to a bit of blank screen, or to an animatic sketch of what's going to be there, and speak it to Garth's requirements. Once the picture has been locked, then we have the final sessions.'

The Vogons

'Vogons are one of the most unpleasant races in the Galaxy – not evil, but bad-tempered, bureaucratic, officious and callous.'

The Guide, *The Hitchhiker's Guide to the Galaxy*

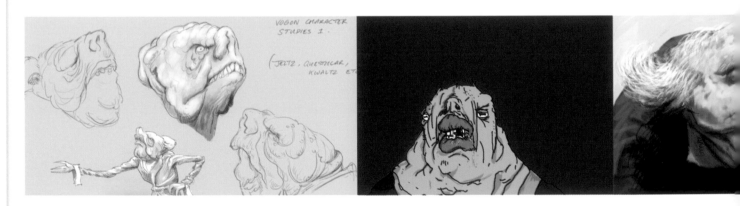

Ford and Arthur have arrived in the toilet of the Vogon ship. Ford introduces Arthur to The Guide, and inserts a Babel Fish in his ear so he can understand alien languages. However, they are captured by a Vogon guard and brought before Jeltz, who reads them some of his poetry before sentencing them to be thrown out of an airlock.

One of the central concepts that endeared Nick and Garth to Disney was the decision to keep things as practical as possible. 'We're not making documentaries,' Nick Goldsmith points out. 'As a film-maker, I am not telling the viewer that a Vogon really exists. Our minds want to be played with. If a good puppeteer puts a sock on his hand, the person watching it ignores that it's a hand in a sock, but just sees the character that's being created.'

In order to create the Vogons, Nick and Garth went back

to Douglas Adams' original novel in which the creatures are described as the backbone of the Galactic Civil Service. 'It all came back to bureaucracy,' Garth says, 'and they were clearly not that dissimilar to the people who run any country, like judges and politicians. We thought that they were like cartoon versions of them, so we looked at satirical, political cartoons.'

Joel Collins lent Garth a book of cartoons by the English political satirist James Gillray, who cast a cynical eye on human nature at the end of the eighteenth century. 'His creations were so grotesque,' Garth points out. 'He had huge, bloated men with bulbous noses, tiny legs, enormous bellies, useless arms and big fat faces. When we looked at them, we realized they *were* the Vogons.'

Garth wasn't simply fascinated by Gillray's designs but also by the lifestyle at the time. 'Wouldn't it be funny,' he recalls thinking, 'if these aliens had waistcoats, cardigans, cuffs and multiple collars rather than lovely metal robes or

The concept design sketches for the Vogons clearly show the influence of cartoonist James Gillray

laser-guided shoulder pads? That almost Dickensian idea seemed to have the feel of stuffy England. Our aliens would be weird, distorted people that you'd recognize from everyday life. Jeltz was inspired by that: the judge's wig was a brilliant addition by one of the conceptual artists who just popped it on top of the Vogon's head.

'The last conceptual element we wanted to include was this new idea that Douglas had come up with for the movie, that if anyone had an original thought on Vogsphere, they got smacked in the face,' Garth continues, 'and earlier in the books he had described how evolution had given up on the Vogons. We combined those ideas, and wanted them to have these slightly smacked faces. They had to have domed noses across the top of their heads, as if you are pushing your face against glass when making faces at children.'

'Garth tapped into lots of different bits and pieces,' Joel recalls. 'He put together picture boards of cows' eyes and illustrated different moods for these characters.'

GILLRAY

James Gillray (1756–1815) was a grand master of visual satire, whose barbed pictures often reflected the public opinion of the time. He came to prominence around the time of the French Revolution in 1789, and his cartoons included a very strong anti-French bias during the Revolution and later the Napoleonic periods. He also cast a weather eye over British politics and the monarchy, particularly poking fun at the Prince Regent – who on occasion would buy every copy of a Gillray print to avoid it being made public.

Creating the Vogons
in the Jim Henson
Creature Shop in
London

To make the Vogon creatures, Nick and Garth turned to the Jim Henson Creature Shop, with whom they had previously worked on various projects. 'Garth showed us the drawings they had done, and gave us a sense of what the Vogons were like,' Creature Shop project supervisor Jamie Courtier explains. 'The Vogon gentry were very decrepit old gentlemen, who wouldn't worry about an egg stain on their front. They wore clothes which had been re-upholstered: they were probably issued with one set of clothes at birth which were let out and altered.'

Garth encouraged Courtier and his colleague Sharon Smith to think as creatively as possible. 'We would sit round a table and have creative workshops over lots of pots of tea,' Courtier recalls. 'He was very clear about the type of characters, rather than the specific designs.'

'What was joyous about creating the Vogons was that they were a bit more edgy and disgusting,' Sharon Smith adds. 'We could get away from being cute or realistic. We've done scary creatures before, but these were foul! You wouldn't want to be anywhere near them – they were smelly and grubby, and didn't care what they looked like.'

Once a design had been agreed, Courtier and Smith created maquettes, small clay models showing the Vogons in three dimensions. The Creature Shop's job then was to turn those models into the 9ft tall creatures seen on screen.

'It's the first time we've made costumes with arms with no human control at all,' Courtier explains. 'The people inside the suits couldn't reach the arms, and anyway they are too thin and long for a human arm to fit inside. A weight support control was needed inside the costumes to get the Vogons going at all – the heads were very big and heavy, and they were being driven by the performer inside the costume. That was a major piece of kit, and we were mass producing them.

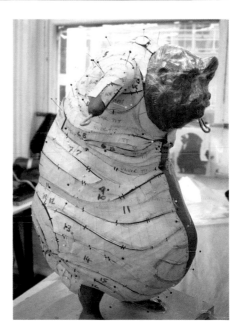

'I made the decision early on to make the skins thick and heavy, to make the movement transmit through the faces when they smiled. However, to make the skin thicker you're using more rubber, you're on the borders of danger with burning out the motors, so we gave them some support to take some of the weight.'

The Performance Control System (PCS), the proprietary technology of the Jim Henson Company, was used to operate the animatronics. 'You have a joy stick in your left hand which has about 10 different controls on it and goes left, right, forward, and back that you use to control the eyes and expressions, ' explains puppeteer Mak Wilson. 'On your right hand you will have a very complicated mitten with lots of potentiometers, and you use that to control lip synch. It's a bit like being a musician, but you've still got to act and portray a character. You're acting and performing at the same time as playing a very complicated banjo.'

The costumes for the Vogons were also created by the Creature Shop, rather than by the costume department, partly because they were needed considerably earlier in the pre-production process than the costume department would normally become involved. 'Kwaltz's costume is quite flouncy,' Sharon Smith notes, 'but all the collarage and cuffs are really made up of lots of tatty old shirts. His cardigan is falling to pieces, and he's got disgusting, smelly old socks with flip-flops. The old backbenchers were in tatty pinstripe suits with grubby shirts, and the minions were inspired by the Gillray cartoons – really greasy long hair, and unkempt in their little uniforms. Rolls of fabric were rolling through the door because of the vastness of each creature. When we had the full dress ready, and we put the performer in the suit, the weight was just phenomenal. Jamie had to reinforce the back structure so that the performer could work in the costume!'

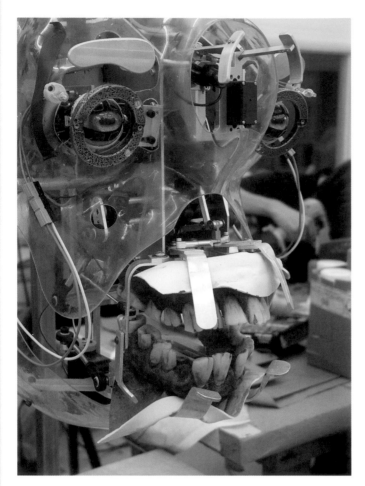

This page: Bringing the Vogons to life
Opposite: Henson Project Supervisor Sharon Smith dresses Kwaltz

'It was pretty clear what the creatures were going to be able to do from the onset,' Jamie Courtier says, 'simply because they were so big. Other people would have to move the arms, or the arms would have to dangle. That wasn't so amiss, because it suited the slovenly Vogon way. We were able to use people's hands inside the gloves for the Councillors when they were sitting down.'

While the banks of Councillors in rows above Jeltz were basic puppets operated by students from the Wimbledon College of Art, Jeltz and Vogon Commander Kwaltz had a considerable amount to do on screen, and therefore required the highest number of people to bring them to life.

'There was one major performer inside,' Courtier explains, 'and then someone outside operating the face on the Control System, one person either side to operate the arms, and at least a couple of dressers standing by to assist the puppeteers. We'd also have an electronics person standing by, who'd deal with more than one person, as would the mechanics and technicians. Finally Peter Elliott, our movement expert, and I would be there to advise on the overall performance.'

Only one body was created for Kwaltz and Jeltz, although each had his own animatronic head. These suits could be operated in two modes. 'They could walk around, when they were inhabited by one of our big guys,' Courtier says, 'and in close-up they had puppeteer Rod Tygner inside them. That's where you want the experience and dexterity that comes from working for the Creature Shop for 15 or more years.'

'The suits were the size of a small Mini, and it was a bit like puppeteering a huge, wet mattress,' recalls Tygner. 'It was really difficult to make that move, but the animatronic and sculpted faces were so beautiful that they brought the creatures alive.'

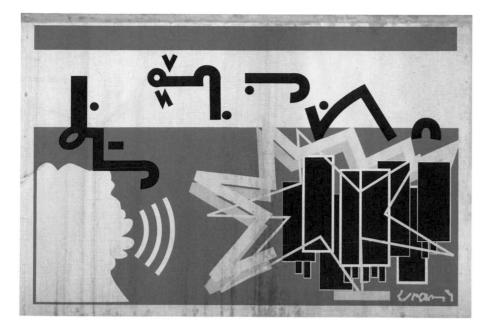

Vogon text

Everything about the Vogons was designed around the idea that 'they're square – they're unhip', Joel Collins explains. 'They're officious paperwork monsters who only care about dotting the i's and getting everything in triplicate. I was adamant that I didn't want to make their language something too visually cheesy. But it would also look wrong if it was written in English.'

After some time wracking his brains, Joel came up with the idea of using shorthand, specifically *Pitmans 2000™*, the language used in offices. However, as he realized, 'that sped things up, which is not what the Vogons are about at all. We counterbalanced the speeding up in shorthand by making each number a line. The number 56 would be ⌗⌗ ⌗⌗ ⌗⌗ ⌗⌗ ⌗⌗ ⌗⌗ ⌗⌗ ⌗⌗ ⌗⌗ ⌗⌗ ⌗⌗ I, so to write a number like 2,000 would take them an hour and a half.'

Graphics designer Anita Dhillon enjoyed using shorthand as the basis of the language. '*Pitmans 2000™* is quite curly, and if you saw it written on posters, you'd think it was Arabic,'

she explains. 'I made it blocky, but we had it checked and it's still readable. Anything that's a sign specifically means something – "destroy", "attack" – and we incorporated that into the Vogon costumes. Kwaltz had badges with all the possibilities: callous, vicious, stupid, idiot, sluggish, revolting, putrid, mouldy, rank and unpleasant. All the soldiers had "Unpleasant" on their shoulders as well. We even made up a font to use on their computers.'

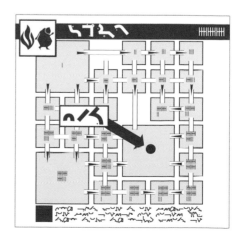

The Vogon fleet

'We didn't want to start with great designs for characters but with a concept for everything,' Garth recalls. 'Most of the concepts were sitting there in the book waiting to be enlarged upon, like Douglas's description of the Vogon ships hanging in the sky in much the same way that bricks don't. Out of that naturally came a Vogon ship.'

'We thought of making it from brick and then concrete,' Joel continues, 'and then from a number of creative discussions, we came up with these Vogon ships which are these massive concrete tower blocks, with hardly any windows. They just have a few doors around the base to allow entry to the interior.'

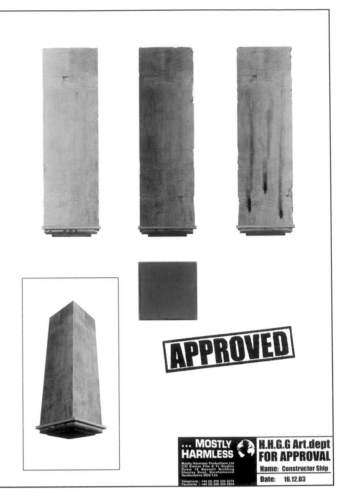

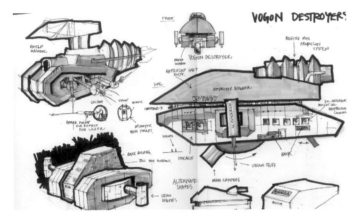

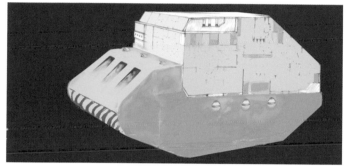

Vogon toilets

The interior sets for all of the Vogon ships had to be huge in order to accommodate the massive creatures, as well as providing space for the puppeteers to operate. 'They were mainly made from plasterwork and steel, although anything that had to be moved for shooting purposes was made from fibreglass,' construction co-ordinator Steve Bohan notes. 'We had to make quite big platforms for the Vogons to stand on, so space was limited. We actually used steel RSJ girders for the main structure, rather than scaffolding. That gave us more room between the walls, so they could be thinner. We built the Council Chamber on Stage 2 at Elstree, which is 50ft high, and it reached to the top of that.'

All the Vogon sets were very similar in design and dressing. 'The brief was a concrete car park,' Kate Beckly recalls. 'The Vogon toilets was one of the sets where their Vogonity was expressed in many ways. It was fun working out what a Vogon toilet would look like, and Vogon tooth-brushes and toothpaste! The prop-making team made loads of brilliant things for the Vogons to use in the Council Chamber – staplers and stamps that worked; fantastic chunky pencils and calculators. And Anita came up with Vogon fire escape signs, and the big snooker board at the end of the room with "Us" and "Them" on it in Vogon.'

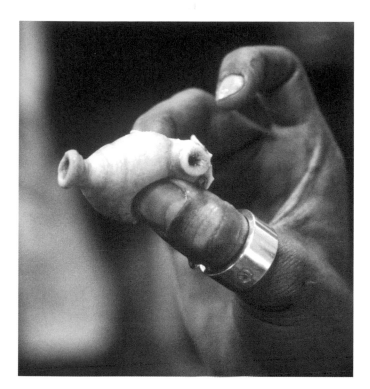

The Babel Fish

The Babel Fish is a combination of a physical effect created by the Creature Shop from Garth's design, and some computer effects courtesy of Cinesite. 'The Babel Fish came right at the end of the building process,' Sharon Smith explains. 'We'd built all these huge creatures and then we came to this tiny thing. Garth's original sketch wasn't changed much – it had lots of little hairs, but there wasn't time to do those.'

'We took the footage and warped it to give it a little bit of animation,' Angus Bickerton adds. 'We couldn't practically achieve the shots where the Fish is forced into Arthur's ear, so we shot the model against bluescreen and then composited it in. We could make a three-dimensional Babel Fish but he's only on screen for three-and-a-half shots, so it's easier to use the real element.'

'The Babel Fish is small, yellow, leech-like, and probably the oddest thing in the Universe.'

The Guide, *The Hitchhiker's Guide to the Universe*

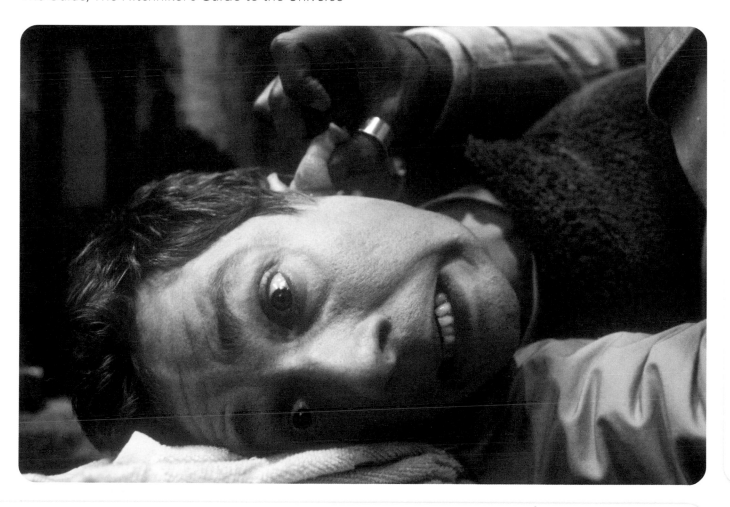

Above: Artwork for
the Constructor
Bridge set
Left: The Vogon
Poetry Book
Opposite: Filming on
the Constructor
Bridge
Below: A Vogon crab
scuttles away from
Jeltz

Vogon poetry

The scene in which Jeltz reads his poetry to his unfortunate captives was one of the last to be shot. One of the advantages of having the Vogons in the studio reacting with the actors was that, although there were logistical problems to be overcome when handling the puppeteering infra-structure around the creatures, not much had to be added in post-production.

'None of it was technically fiddly,' Garth Jennings recalls, 'because we'd built all the set that we were going to see, and we didn't have to worry too much about making allowances for bluescreen work. That sequence went exactly as I'd storyboarded it, and it's so lovely when that happens. The camera goes up the ramp, comes round the side of this thing and just when you wonder who the hell this is, Jeltz is revealed, like a Bond villain, smashing the crab.'

Opposite: Torture by Poetry
This page: Some of Prostetnic Vogon Jeltz's previous victims

The Constructor Bridge set included various dead aliens who had succumbed to the Vogon poetry. 'They had to be sculpted and look like real creatures,' Creature Shop producer Tracy Lenon notes. 'Originally there was going to be someone inside the plinth with a bit of life left, but they decided they wanted them to be dead. We were given descriptions of various alien races from Douglas's books, and made them to those specifications.'

The poetry reading itself was one of the highlights for Lenon. 'All the eyelines were right, and so was the temperament,' she recalls. 'Everything about the performance was just as you expected it should be, and the camera moved at the right time with Jeltz's movements. He really was living and breathing. I've seen some great puppetry and great performances, but that captured everything.'

'Resistance is useless!'

Vogon soldier, *The Hitchhiker's Guide to the Galaxy*

Clearing the trash

Although some of the smaller Vogon sets were created by altering the geography of one of the larger sets, the airlock from which Ford and Arthur are thrown into space was a separate build. 'The airlock would also be where the Vogons let all their rubbish out,' Kate Beckly points out, 'so we encrusted it with debris of their paperwork and the sort of stuff you'd find embedded in an empty skip.'

The Heart of Gold

'It would have been a great deal simpler and more practical to build the cabin as an ordinary three-dimensional oblong room, but then the designers would have got miserable.'

The Hitchhiker's Guide to the Galaxy

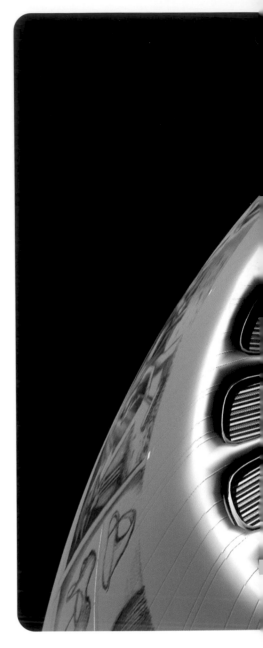

Just as they are about to die, Ford and Arthur are rescued by the Heart of Gold, a ship fitted with the new Infinite Improbability Drive, which was stolen by Galactic President Zaphod Beeblebrox. The ship's robot, Marvin, takes them to meet Zaphod and his girlfriend Trillian – who improbably turns out to be the girl that Arthur met and lost at the party in Islington.

'Designing spaceships is extremely hard,' Garth Jennings maintains. Or at least, as he discovered during the pre-viz process, creating a spaceship that was right for this movie was hard. 'It's easy to design a groovy spaceship – we've come up with some of the most amazing spaceships you've ever seen. But when we looked at them, they could have been in any film. They didn't look very Hitchhikerish.'

As ever, Nick, Garth and Joel returned to first principles.

'With every aspect of this film, we were trying to come up with something that was loyal to the intention and the idea of the original books, but was going to be our personal take on it,' Garth points out. 'The most important thing about the Heart of Gold is the Infinite Improbability Drive, so we decided to make that the be-all and end-all of the ship. The Drive basically works by random factoring, so we thought about roulette wheels, and that led to a design like a giant cone going down to infinity. The most economical way to contain the Drive would be in a sphere. We realized it was staring us in the face that the Vogons were square, and the Heart of Gold was round. We started to tart it up again, but it started to look like just another spaceship, and we realized that the surface of it was lacking personality. It had to have personality, and it had to be unique. At its heart is a cup of tea, so we decided to make the ship completely out of porcelain, which is the wrong thing to make a whole spaceship from!'

The exterior shots were created as computer graphics by Cinesite. 'The Heart of Gold is almost a perfect sphere, with a shiny ceramic surface,' Angus Bickerton points out. 'That lent itself automatically to being made in this way. Having a 6ft reflective sphere in the middle of a studio floor to film as a miniature would have been a nightmare!'

Right and below:
Early ideas for the
Heart of Gold

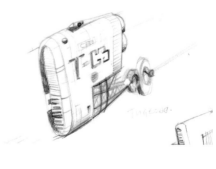

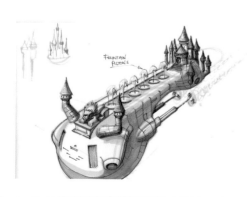

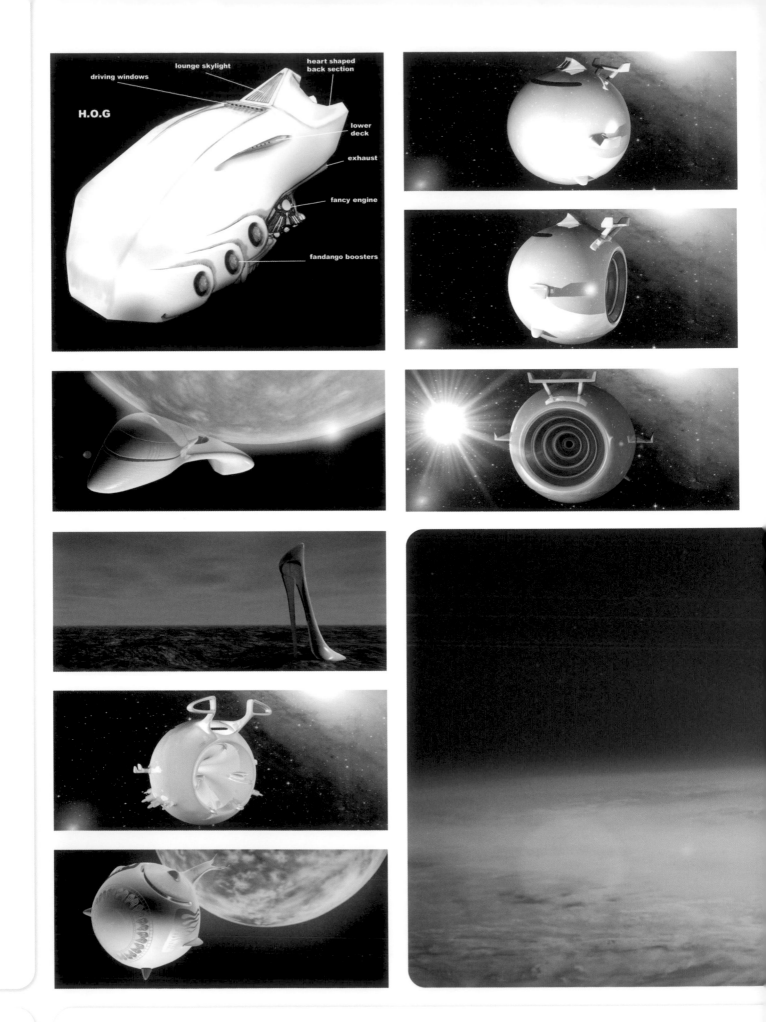

APPROVED

The first day of shooting on the Heart of Gold coincided with the anniversary of Douglas Adams's death. In the callsheet for 11 May 2004, Robbie Stamp wrote:

'It was exactly three years ago today that Douglas Adams died unexpectedly of a heart attack. As a mark of respect for Douglas and his family we will be observing a minute's silence after Line Up (Approx. 0800) and then we'll gather outside stage 2 for a cast and crew photograph to celebrate the making of the movie that Douglas himself wanted to happen. We would like as many people involved as possible to be in the photograph. I know he would have been delighted by what is finally now happening.'

'Garth's brief for the interior of the Heart of Gold was to have a space that was shootable from every angle,' Joel Collins recalls. 'Wherever he put the camera, he wanted to see an interesting space. A lot of sets are designed with big open spaces, but what we had to do here was create something that gave him a good dynamic shot from every angle. It was painful to try to do. How do you visualize something that has to be so multi-layered for different angles with just one sketch?'

Because of the complex nature of the set, all the construction departments had to work simultaneously on the build. Joel and the Art Department worked for a long time to come up with the design, and the production designer remembers that 'the Heart of Gold console looked like a sausage. It had no logic other than pure fear and frustration of design.'

'They were lovely designs to work from,' models super-

visor Mark Mason comments. 'It was tricky because of all the different curves. The panel is made from plywood, bonded together in the curves. There were more than 2,000 holes drilled to hold the perspex balls, which were sandblasted and lit from behind.'

'The boys had sore fingers after wiring all the lights,' electrical gaffer Eddie Night laughs. 'There were over 3,000 in total on the set, all wired individually.'

'We weren't supposed to keep the lights on for more than six minutes at a time, because the set might burn down,' Nick Goldsmith recalls. 'It was a big impressive-looking set that we designed to work in one piece, which it did. It was an engineering feat in itself. The construction team and the lighting team were up against it to get it built in time.'

'We prefabricated material in the workshops for five weeks, and built the set in nine or so,' construction co-ordinator Steve Bohan says. 'It was such a complicated set

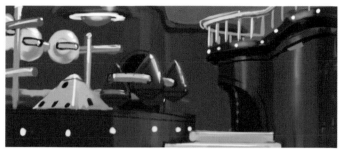

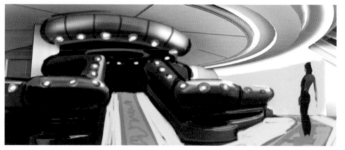

for the Art Department to draw that we couldn't really change it once we got started. Joel was very good at incorporating ideas if we thought of a quicker way of cutting the cloth, but once we were under way, if we changed one part of the set, it would move things somewhere else. It wasn't like the Vogon sets, made from square walls: the geometric shapes in the Heart of Gold meant if you made one piece shorter, it had repercussions elsewhere. Every department was sitting on each other's shoulders for the last two weeks.'

Above: The Heart of Gold under construction
Right: Various concept designs for its interior

INT. H.O.G. RECEIVING RM

1.235

Racing against time to complete building the interior of the Heart of Gold

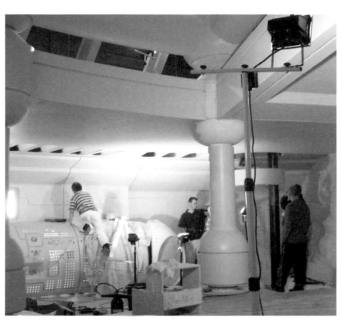

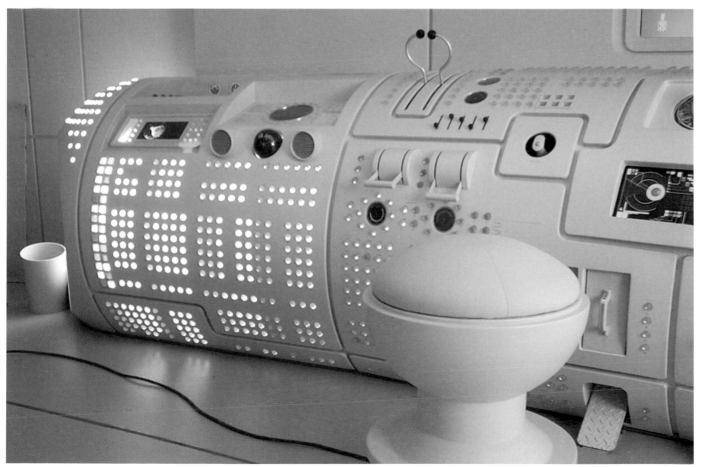

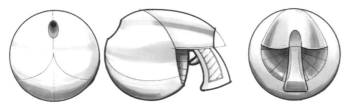

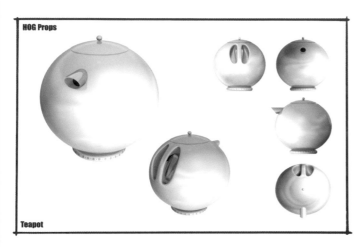

Various props designed for the Heart of Gold, including (right) the laser bread knife

SHARE AND ENJOY

Model makers Asylum and set decorator Kate Beckly worked together to create the fantastic gadgets that littered the Heart of Gold. 'We'd find ourselves going round and round in circles,' Kate recalls. 'You'd expect the kitchen to be state of the art, but then if you've got a Sensomatic machine which senses what you need, you've got no requirement for lots of fantastic gadgets. In the bathroom there were some bits of dressing that wouldn't really be there I suppose, but a toothbrush looks kind of funny and out of place in a high-tech spaceship,'

'Everyone wanted to make a mark, and I was very strong about reining them in,' Joel Collins notes. 'It was better to do nothing than over-egg it. The whole film is not over-designed or over-propped. But it was hard with so many creative people involved.'

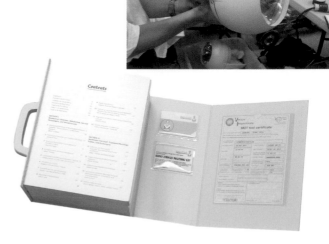

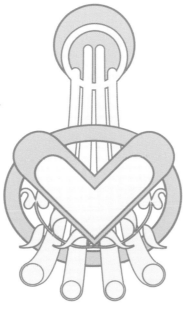

Could the Heart of Gold logo (**right**) have been inspired in part by a rejected design (**above**) for the rear of the ship itself?

'You think you've got problems?

What are you supposed to do if you are a manically depressed robot? No, don't bother to answer that, I'm fifty thousand times more intelligent than you and even I don't know the answer. It gives me a headache just trying to think down to your level.'

Marvin, *The Hitchhiker's Guide to the Galaxy*

Opposite: Assorted concept designs for Marvin

Marvin

'Marvin was one of the first things that we designed for the film,' Garth Jennings notes. 'The script was still being worked on so we could concentrate on the characters. He started out as a spider chart: Marvin – paranoid – weight of the world on his shoulders – brain the size of a planet – everyone looks down on him. We looked at that, and really that drew itself. He had a huge head with a permanent hard-done-by look. The book says he's made of brushed steel, but I didn't feel we had to be totally loyal to the text. The pure essence is there. The book says he has these upturned triangles for eyes, which we could use in the same way that Japanese design uses abstract elements to create a sense of character. It was funny because he was someone with a complex stuck in a cartoon-type costume. There's nothing sadder than that – he's so cute and sweet-looking, which balances out the depressed side of him.'

'When you take these iconic characters, you are never going to satisfy everyone's sense of the character they have in their mind,' Robbie Stamp points out. 'You have to design something that has such integrity and works so beautifully that maybe it isn't the Marvin that people had in their heads, but when they leave the cinema they have to admit that "that definitely was a Marvin!"'

'The design of Marvin was locked down when we came on board,' Creature Shop supervisor Jamie Courtier says. 'We took it forward into maquette stage. We then overlaid an image of a little person, which coincidentally was Warwick Davis, and to our surprise it fitted him almost like a glove.'

Davis originally came to the Creature Shop to discuss one of the short actors represented by his Willow Agency taking the role, but ended up playing Marvin himself. 'I thought the design was gorgeous,' he says. 'He's a piece of art that moves around.'

Warwick Davis
prepares to become
Marvin

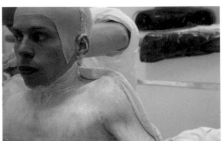

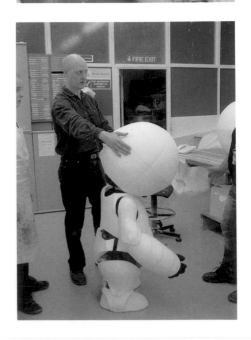

WORKING WITH A BIG HEAD

Getting Marvin on and off set was sometimes a problem. 'We would dress Warwick off camera, only to find he was barricaded out of the set by lighting stands and screens,' his dresser Paul Jomain recalls. 'Suddenly a forceful "Are you ready?" would come our way. It took a long while before people realized that Marvin's large head wasn't going to squeeze miraculously between the stands. It was like walking with a very large baby – my colleague Nicola and I would grab both his hands and walk him back in case he fell. Warwick's vision was via a small camera mounted in the black line around his head. That was connected to a monitor mounted inside the head, but if the camera was shooting from above we could remove his chin panel and he could see the ground!'

Although at one stage the size of the head section was made smaller, in order to make the suit more practical, the final version of Marvin is identical to the sketches that Garth took to the Creature Shop. 'In the course of the build, we had to re-expand the head size,' Courtier recalls, 'but when you expand a sphere by the small amount of 15 per cent, the weight goes up something like 60 per cent. That made it enormously hard technically, because we then had to invent a weight support system which allowed Warwick to control the head using his own head, but allowed the weight of the head to be supported on his harness.'

Marvin was created from lightweight fibreglass, neoprene, nylon webbing and aluminium for the engineering parts, and in total weighed around 56lbs, two-thirds of Warwick's 6st body weight. 'It was a very nervous moment when he put the suit on for the first time,' Creature Shop head of design Sharon Smith remembers.

'It was very demanding,' Warwick agrees. 'I've done many films and worn many different costumes throughout my career, and I thought this would be a straightforward costume that I could put on in about 20 minutes, and take off at lunchtime. But as the build went on, it dawned on me that this really wasn't going to be quite as easy as I had anticipated. I started off working in a rehearsal room with a video camera, but then I was introduced to Peter Elliott, who was an inspiration.'

Elliott encouraged Warwick to think of Marvin as a character, and to find a performance which he could then create using the suit. 'Before that I'd been operating the suit as a puppeteer might,' Warwick says. 'That wasn't right. It had to come from the emotion within me, which would come through. It looked incredibly natural, and went with the dialogue Marvin was saying.'

Marvin looked perfectly at home on the Heart of Gold, his round head mirroring the spherical shape of the ship. 'When we designed him, he was basically shouting at us that this was how the Heart of Gold should look,' Garth Jennings remembers. 'He was saying, "Look, I'm part of all this stuff!"'

'Life? Don't talk to me about life.'

'I think you ought to know I'm feeling very depressed.'

Marvin, *The Hitchhiker's Guide to the Galaxy*

Left: Taking the stowaways to the bridge
Below left: Arriving with the Vogons
Below: Descending to the organic lifeforms' level

Arthur shoves Zaphod's hand off his shoulder. Oddly, Zaphod reacts with a smile. And then — his head shoots all the up way revealing a second head that lives somewhere under his chin.

Stage direction from *The Hitchhiker's Guide to the Galaxy* script

Zaphod's second head

Zaphod's second head, which began as a one-line joke for the original radio series, was one of the key conceptual areas to be worked out before filming could commence. 'Before Nick and Garth came on board, I think that it was actually Jay Roach who had come up with this new idea that Zaphod's head springs up from around his neck,' visual effects supervisor Angus Bickerton explains. 'His character has separated into two halves, and the alter ego – the side you wouldn't want your mum to meet – is hidden underneath that pashmina along with the third arm. Consequently he doesn't have to appear in every shot.'

While the third arm was achieved partly by compositing in footage of another arm, and partly by using a puppet arm manipulated by one of the Creature Shop puppeteers, a second head was harder to devise. Nick and Garth had experimented with some simple two-dimensional processes, superimposing the second head over footage of Sam Rockwell with his head thrown back. 'That limits how much the character can move around,' Angus points out.

'We asked Sam back, shot him against bluescreen, and aligned that exactly to the original shot. If he was looking to the right, we would line him up exactly, and we could match-move the little bits of natural movement. However, when he starts to move around the screen to any large degree, there's no way we can match-move it.'

Angus and his team therefore used a technique called cyberscanning (which works in a similar way to an MRI scan at a hospital) to prepare a three-dimensional version of Sam Rockwell's head with his mouth in various different positions. Using Maya 3D software, they were then able to animate the head between those different positions, so that the computer-generated head was 'talking'. That was then matched into the footage of Sam's performance as the first head, and the whole scene was then lit so that the transition between the two-dimensional and three-dimensional heads was seamless.

'We spent a lot of time working on this at the beginning,' Angus comments, 'because we realized that Zaphod's second head is one of the signature elements of Hitchhikers, something that everyone remembers.'

'For the scenes when the second head was going to make an appearance, Sam Rockwell had to move around the set with his neck exposed, his head tilted right back,' Robbie Stamp recalls. 'It looked pretty painful to be honest. Somebody else read his lines for him so that everybody else in the scene had the right dialogue to react to. I take my hat off to Sam's neck muscles!'

Zaphod's second head at various stages of development.

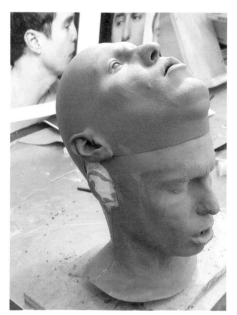

Vogon Command Headquarters

'I don't have ideas, Madam Vice President. I just do what I do.'

Vogon Commander Kwaltz, *The Hitchhiker's Guide to the Galaxy*

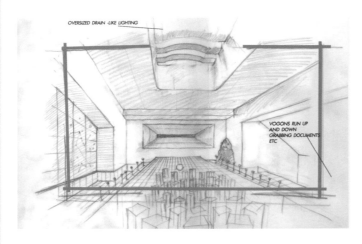

OVERSIZED DRAIN -LIKE LIGHTING

VOGONS RUN UP AND DOWN GRABBING DOCUMENTS ETC

In the Vogon Command Headquarters, Vice-president Questular becomes increasingly annoyed at the bureaucratic machinations of Commander Kwaltz, knowing that Zaphod has been relying on the Vogons' lack of initiative to give him a head start in his quest to find the Ultimate Computer...

'Whenever we were creating a moment for the script, we tried to think of the un-*Star Wars™* way of doing it,' scriptwriter Karey Kirkpatrick remembers. 'What would *Star Wars™* do at this point in the story? Whatever it was, we would do the opposite. If *Star Wars™* would have a bunch of ships leaping into hyperspace in pursuit, we'd have a bunch of ships sitting there, waiting for hyperspace clearance.'

The Vogon Council Chamber is at the heart of the Vogon bureaucracy seen in the movie, and was one of the most populated sets of the entire film, with Commander Kwaltz and the Councillors at the War Table, all of whom were fully-operational Vogons. With approximately four people needed to bring each to life, it meant that there were a large number of puppeteers and Creature Shop personnel who needed to be accommodated on set – and kept out of sight during filming.

During the pre-production design phase, Joel Collins worked closely with the Creature Shop to ensure that those on set would have everything that they needed. Joel had worked for Hensons some years previously, and took an office in their Camden Lock headquarters during part of pre-production to make sure that everything went smoothly.

'We had meetings at Elstree Studios while the chamber and the table were being built,' Jamie Courtier explains. 'With long-sighted speculation as to what we might need, we had removable panels made for the top surface of the table in order to have puppeteers underneath operating the hands through a hole in the side.'

Zaphod's Vice-president, who clearly has more than one reason for pursuing him halfway across the galaxy, was a new character created for the film. Anna Chancellor is immediately recognizable for her role as Duckface in the classic comedy *Four Weddings and a Funeral*, and had both the height necessary not to be totally dwarfed by the Vogons and yet still demonstrate their incredible stature, as well as the acting talent to reveal her unrequited love and pining for Zaphod.

'The first day we shot the Vogons I thought was going to be a nightmare, with the Vogons' animatronics not working,' observes Nick Goldsmith. 'But it went without a hitch. We were on schedule – the Vogons all did what they had to do with no technical malfunctions.'

Courtier recalls an early production meeting in which he boasted that the eight minutes downtime needed for animatronic repairs during an earlier movie that one producer was involved with, was far more than would be needed on Hitchhikers. 'It was one of the most astonishingly glitch-free animatronic projects that I've been on set for,' he notes. 'I don't think we had any downtime due to burnt-out motors.'

'That was a very pleasant surprise,' Nick concludes. 'It all came down to very good co-ordination by the production manager and the ADs [assistant directors], making sure that we had enough puppeteers and enough back-up staff to make sure that everything worked.'

Top: Preparing the Vogon Command Headquarters
Above left: One of the Vogon Commanders
Left: The Vogon Runner

'You mean to tell me you carved up your brain so you could become President so you would get invited to the launching ceremony of this ship so you could steal it so you could go to Magrathea which, according to most sane people, doesn't even exist?'

Ford Prefect, *The Hitchhiker's Guide to the Galaxy*

Zaphod's Quest

Zaphod explains to Ford and Arthur that he is searching for the Ultimate Question. The massive computer Deep Thought worked out that the Ultimate Answer to Life, the Universe and Everything is 42, but wasn't capable of calculating the Ultimate Question. It provided the specifications for the Ultimate Computer – but the computer records have been deleted, and no-one knows what it is called...

'The design of Deep Thought came from one of the mad sessions that Garth and I had,' Joel Collins says. 'We were trying to find something that had a Buddha-esque style, or was like something you'd find on a totem pole. We didn't want it to look like a Buddha, but we wanted it to have that feeling. Art director Phil Sims thrashed out forty or so ideas from the rough sketches I made, and the more weird it became, the more right it seemed. We had one that was a big sculpted character sitting on a toilet with his head in his hands, a bit like Rodin's *The Thinker*. But it was too funny. Garth wanted a big head, and there is a Thinker-esque element to the final design. Ironically, although it isn't based on one of Garth's drawings, it does look like something he

might have done. It came together like a fine art piece, and it seemed to have something of a personality, even though it was inanimate. It always looks like it's about to move.'

TELL US THE ANSWER

Although the computer model was enhanced by computer graphics at Cinesite, the area around Deep Thought's temple was constructed and appropriately redressed for the three different times it appears in the film. The area is surrounded by pristine jungle when the philosophers ask their question, but the trees have been cut down by the time that Deep Thought has completed his task. When Zaphod reaches his goal at the end of the film, there is utter desolation. 'We had fun thinking of ideas for the time when Fook and Lunkwill return to get the Answer,' set decorator Kate Beckly says. 'The crowd had various items of Deep Thought merchandising like Deep Thought shaped ice-lollies and T-shirts.'

THINK DEEP

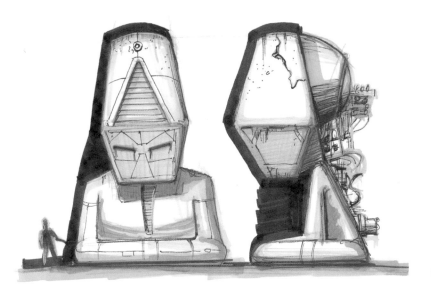

Early designs and artwork for Deep Thought

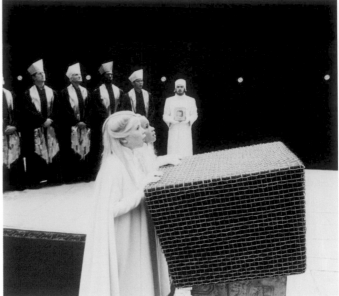

Above: Filming Fook and Lunkwill's audience with Deep Thought
Opposite bottom: Note Deep Thought's guards carrying functioning Point of View guns

Executive producer Robbie Stamp admits to a bit of trepidation when he heard that Garth intended to cast children as the two philosophers, Fook and Lunkwill. 'I thought people would put two and two together and make five,' he says. '"Disney are casting kids in Hitchhikers, but there are no kids in Hitchhikers!" But when we looked at the tapes of the auditions, Garth and Nick and I quite separately liked the same pair of children – they have this slightly otherworldly, strange element to them, and when you add in the female voice of Deep Thought we're using, we've moved a long way away from what could essentially have been written as a Monty Python sketch.'

'It was difficult to design Fook and Lunkwil, because we didn't initially know if they were going to be children or adults,' costume designer Sammy Sheldon recalls. 'I also had to design them in a way that was subliminally mouselike. They couldn't just look like little mice.'

Sammy worked with Garth to create costumes that suggested the idea of mice, without using steel bands or other items 'that would make them look like they've walked off the set of *Star Wars™*.' Jewellery on the characters' heads gave the impression of ears, while the top parts of their cloaks were constructed so that it appeared as if their hands just came out of the front of their chests.

The Infinite Improbability Drive is a wonderful new method of crossing interstellar distances in a mere nothingth of a second, without all that tedious mucking about in hyperspace. The principle of generating small amounts of *finite* improbability by simply **hooking the logic circuits of a Bambleweeny 57 Sub-Meson Brain to an atomic vector plotter suspended in a strong Brownian Motion producer (say a nice hot cup of tea)** were, of course, well understood — and such generators were often used to break the ice at parties, by making all the molecules in the hostess's undergarments simultaneously leap one foot to the left, in accordance with the Theory of Indeterminacy.

Many respectable physicists said that they weren't going to stand for that sort of thing, partly because it was a debasement of science, but mostly **because they didn't get invited to those sorts of parties.**

Another thing they couldn't stand was the perpetual failure they encountered in trying to construct a machine that could generate the infinite improbability field needed to flip a spaceship across the mind-paralysing distances between the furthest stars, and in the end they grumpily announced that such a machine was virtually impossible.

Then, one day, a student, who had been left to sweep up the lab after a particularly unsuccessful party, found himself reasoning this way: **If, he thought to himself, such a machine is a virtual impossibility, then, it must logically be a finite improbability!** So, all I have to do in order to make one, is to work out exactly how improbable it is, then feed that figure into the finite improbability generator, give it **a fresh cup of really hot tea...** and turn it on.

He did this and was rather startled to discover that he managed to create the long-sought-after golden Infinite Improbability Generator out of thin air. It startled him even more when, just after he was awarded the Galactic Institute's Prize for Extreme Cleverness, he got lynched by a rampaging mob of respectable physicists who had finally realised that **the one thing they really couldn't stand was a smartass.**

The Hitchhiker's Guide to the Galaxy

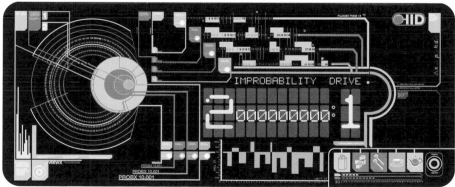

The Infinite Improbability Drive

To escape the pursuing Vogons, Zaphod activates the Infinite Improbability Drive, but unfortunately the Heart of Gold doesn't end up where he wants it to be...

'The Infinite Improbability Drive is one of the most brilliant ideas for story telling,' Garth laughs. 'It's a gigantic contrivance machine, and I love that,' Karey Kirkpatrick adds. 'In its simplest terms, this movie is the story of "the one that got away", and using the laws of infinite improbability to give you a second chance. We had to get away with a few convenient contrivances.'

In the movie, the Heart of Gold makes a few more jumps using the IID on the way to Magrathea than in previous versions of the story. 'We were in a position where we had to keep creating the effects of going through an Infinite Improbability field,' Karey continues. 'We had a number of different versions, and we were constantly looking for the one that felt the most clever and random. At one point I had all the guts of the ship turn inside out, so everything was encased in wires. Another idea was to have them made from computer wire-frame, and that evolved into the idea that they were all knitted.'

'I had been working on Tim Burton's stop motion movie *The Corpse Bride* before I started on Hitchhikers,' Sean Mathiesen recalls. 'Then I spent several months working on the pre-viz, and during that discussed the fact that I had done stop-motion in the past. When I left college, I used to do the station IDs for MTV which were all very raw. Garth wanted the animated sequence also to be very raw, and shockingly different from everything else – and that's what I had done right out of college.'

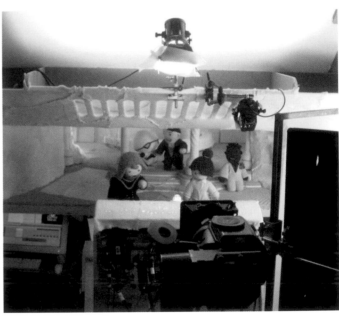

Above: Constructing the puppets and preparing them for the woolen sequence
Opposite bottom left: Storyboards for the transition from wool to reality
Opposite bottom right: Arthur mid-transition

Garth made sketches of the way he envisaged the characters in their woollen state, and passed them to Sean. 'Joel introduced me to Trevor Collins, who was a theatrical costume-maker and knitter, and I then built a foam maquette of Garth's drawings,' Sean explains. 'Trevor built a knitted skin to go on those, while I sent illustrations and photos to an armature builder to make a metal ball-and-socket skeleton, and then checked that the knitted skin would fit over those. I then made a denser foam for the musculature that fits over the metal skeleton, then fitted the loose skin on top, sewed it up, and sewed the eyes and other details so that they could blink. I also rigged up the lips so the puppets of Zaphod and Trillian could synchronize with the dialogue that Sam and Zooey had recorded. At the same time, the guys at the model makers, Asylum, built a perfect miniature version of the Heart of Gold which we covered in a good textured wool that would really show up on film.'

It took about two weeks to design and sculpt the puppets, and then about a further five to build both them and the set. 'I was literally sewing on the last of the eyeballs as we were finishing lighting the set and setting down the characters to start filming,' Sean recalls.

The sequence is highly unusual and a good example of the use in the movie of low-tech ideas alongside state-of-the-art computer graphics designed by Cinesite. 'It's a real throwback to an old style of filmmaking,' Sean notes. 'There's something really tactile in wool and puppets that you can get a handle on, which you wouldn't be able to if it was all done digitally. With puppets you can do things that seem improbable.'

FLOLLOP

'The most famous Infinite Improbability Drive effect is probably "I think I'm a sofa",' Karey Kirkpatrick notes, and the sofas in the film have a particular resonance for both director and production designer, since they are based on the ones that they were using throughout production of the film.

'We arrived at Elstree and were overawed by our offices,' Joel Collins remembers. 'In mine, there was this small two-seater fake leather Chesterfield sofa. When we were looking at the sofas for the Heart of Gold, Garth said, "I want that sofa in your office!" so we measured it, drew a proper construction blueprint of it and then had two of them made at Asylum. That sofa sat in front of me for weeks, and now it's been immortalized on screen!'

THE IID HISTORY

Around the nose of the Heart of Gold is an illustrated history of the Infinite Improbability Drive. 'It's part of our whole idea that you can scratch the surface of any element of this film, and you'll discover something deeper,' Joel Collins explains. 'The only way to envisage the history was to draw it, so Turlo, who's a great fan of the books, spent 12 weeks drawing it up. Everyone's in there, including Douglas holding a glass of wine, Garth, Nick and Robbie.'

A NICE CUP OF TEA

Although many of the effects for the film are created within the computers at Cinesite, many traditional special effects techniques are in use as well. 'Garth enjoys finding a practical and achievable solution to a problem,' Angus Bickerton says. 'He gets a kick out of doing that and I think he feels that sometimes it makes a more creative solution.'

The odd shapes that the Heart of Gold adopts during its transitions through the Infinite Improbability Drive were originally going to be achieved with computer graphics. 'We said to Garth, "What if we shot those elements for real and cut them together as a 2-D effect?"' Andy Fowler says. Accordingly Angus spent time in a studio photographing everyday objects like a teacup, which were then fed into the computer and composited alongside the effects that could only be done with a computer, combining reality and fantasy in a seamless mix.

Viltvodle 6

'Almighty Arkleseizure, we lift our noses, clogged and unblown in reverence to you. Send the handkerchief, oh blessed one, so that it may wipe us clean.'

Humma Kavula, *The Hitchhiker's Guide to the Galaxy*

The IID has brought the Heart of Gold to Viltvodle 6, where Zaphod's former political opponent Humma Kavula is now the high priest of a religion dedicated to the Great Green Arkleseizure. Humma gives Zaphod the co-ordinates for Magrathea, but demands that Zaphod bring him back a gun invented by Deep Thought...

Film screenplays often follow a similar basic structure. In Act I, the characters and their motivations are introduced. In Act 2, various difficulties conspire to get in the characters' way so that they can't achieve their goals. In Act 3, they find what they are looking for, and triumph over their adversities. The problem that Douglas Adams faced when turning the radio and book versions of Hitchhikers into a film screenplay, was that the story he had told didn't confirm to those three acts. Act I saw everyone introduced and brought together

on board The Heart of Gold, but then almost immediately – in a brief, post-credits one-line joke at the end of episode 2 of the radio series, or one four-page chapter in the book – they arrive at their goal, the legendary planet of Magrathea, by-passing Act 2 and its attendant complications entirely.

Douglas devised a solution which became the template for the screenplay for the movie – use the IID to send the Heart of Gold somewhere else along the way. Although this solved the screenplay's structural problems, there were still logistical difficulties to be dealt with before the film entered production.

'The Viltvodle sequence is a very good example of the process that went into the making of this movie,' screenwriter Karey Kirkpatrick says. 'We had to cut the production costs on the sequence. Garth came up with the idea that since there was a Guide entry that said the guys on Viltvodle had invented the aerosol before the wheel, because they were

50-armed creatures, the entire planet would be covered in mist. That would eliminate the need for background shots and infinite horizons that would be phenomenally expensive to create in post-production. Instead we have this moody, foggy planet which is inspired by one line from the book.'

'In the script Viltvodle was originally described as "Las Vegas on steroids",' Garth recalls. 'When we were looking at all the creatures that we were going to put into this planet, we realized that they would be too expensive to make for just fleeting glances at them. But now with this terrible ozone problem on Viltvodle, it's just fog and lights, and everything moves in and out of the shadows. It's more like the beginning of *ET*™ when they're running around in the forest. We also wanted it to be a different beat in the story — we've just been on this blindingly white spaceship, and the Vogons are living in a multi-storey car park, so now we cut to this foggy planet with these hairy slinkies crawling along!'

Above: Humma Kavula's followers gather in the Temple
Left: One of the more unusual inhabitants of Viltvodle VI

The foggy atmosphere meant that the creature budget could literally be cut in half. 'We couldn't afford all those creatures – we kept designing them, but we couldn't afford them,' Garth laughs. 'So when we had half the budget, we halved the creatures, and cut them off at the knee! That sequence was technically challenging because, of course, since we'd only made half the creatures, we had to be very careful how we shot them. We thought we'd got it, but when we went back and looked at it, we'd made the best of a bad day. We knew it could be better, so we went back and reshot it.'

All the various departments had input into the different aliens required for the sequence. 'A lot of the characters were propelled by humour,' Creature Shop project supervisor Jamie Courtier points out. 'There were some creatures we made which were just huge balls of fur, but unfortunately they hit the skids when the Fire Department drenched the set, and they became like little sponges!'

'We took Garth's sketches, and worked them up into finished designs,' Sharon Smith adds. 'It was a mad couple of days thinking of clever value-for-money tricks. The Charlie Corkscrews were meant to be shadows in the background, but they kept coming more and more to the foreground and getting increasingly complex.'

The costume and make-up departments created some of the other aliens. 'I wish there had been more of that to do, because that was such good fun,' make-up designer Liz Tyne says. 'Garth said that he didn't want any aliens we had seen before. He used the Beatles animated film *Yellow Submarine* as a reference point, so we tried to bring inanimate objects into human form. There was a block head, who had a chin block with a moustache, with pins sticking out of the top, so he looked like the blocks we used to keep pins on. There's a guy whose nose is a torch, another who has got CDs for ears.'

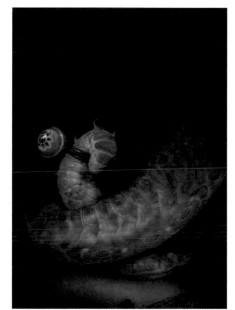

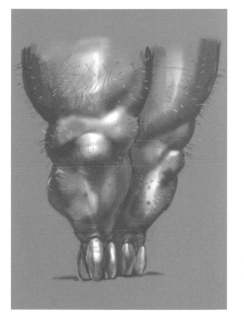

Costume designer Sammy Sheldon saw her challenge as 'making the people on Viltvodle fit in with some of the creatures that were designed. We made some people look odd by using period pieces of costume mixed with modern stuff, and changing their body shapes with padding. I made 15 new outfits using random colours that would work in that smoky environment. One lady is made out of red shiny Lycra with black burned-out netting over it, so there's a two-tone effect which looked like flesh with bits sticking out. Some of them were based on sea creatures or birds – one person was pigeon-chested with a big bottom and very fine feathers up and down, an Edwardian jacket over the top and some really mad goggles. There had to be some detail to make all of them believable.'

The Viltvodle sequences weren't shot on the normal sound stages at Elstree, but at a special set built at Frogmore Studios. 'We tested the smoke over and over, so that we knew the levels were safe enough to stand in,' Joel Collins remembers. 'Even something seemingly simple was tested and tried.'

'The whole flooring was made of seas of spent aerosol cans and pools of water,' Kate Beckly notes. 'We had about 11,000 cans there – my prop men loved me for that – and we were heaving about tons of road scalpings, the bits of tarmac that are left when they dig up the road. It was quite a

challenge to light, because with the fog, all the light is lost.'

'Garth isn't a beauty director,' Nick Goldsmith explains. 'Making something beautiful is not necessarily as high up on his agenda as making the viewer completely and utterly care about the characters.'

BOYS AND THEIR TOYS

Creature Shop producer Tracy Lenon recalls one creature that received an unexpected makeover on set. 'We created some remote control creatures that were meant to run around the set and interact with the other creatures. Garth hadn't seen one of them working before, and asked if he could have a go operating it. It was a shiny blue, perfect plastic little creature with a headlight at the front. Garth got very excited and sent it through a test patch of gravel – and it went flying, and the gravel grazed the ring around it. It wasn't shiny any more!'

MARCHING ON ITS STOMACH

Once all the various aliens were in make up, they still had ordinary human requirements like food, which led to a very odd sight for Executive producer Robbie Stamp on one of his regular set visits. 'It was one of those real bittersweet moments for me when I arrived on the set on a Saturday morning, and there were all these amazing characters queuing up at the catering truck and doing crossword puzzles. Douglas would have loved that moment.'

Designs for the exterior of the Temple, based around a 3D sculpt of Douglas Adams's nose!

The Temple of Humma Kavula

'We only invented where we had to invent,' Robbie Stamp comments. 'Whenever Karey had a problem with the screenplay, he was able to go back to the radio series, or the book or indeed to a host of back story ideas and new potential plotlines. For example, a major new character for Act 2 of the film was Humma Kavula. One of the options was for him to be a missionary, although in one of the earlier versions he was going to be a nightclub owner. We decided to go with the missionary idea.'

'We always tried to start with clues from the original work, and then go mental from that,' Garth says. 'Sometimes that would produce very obvious designs. We realized that Humma Kavula's temple should be very recognizably Earthly. The quote from the Guide at the start – "Things are not always what they seem" – applies to the whole film. Everyone walks into the Temple, and there's a hymn being sung. A guy with a perm and ridiculous glasses is talking about the nose of the Great Arkleseizure, and it's only later revealed that

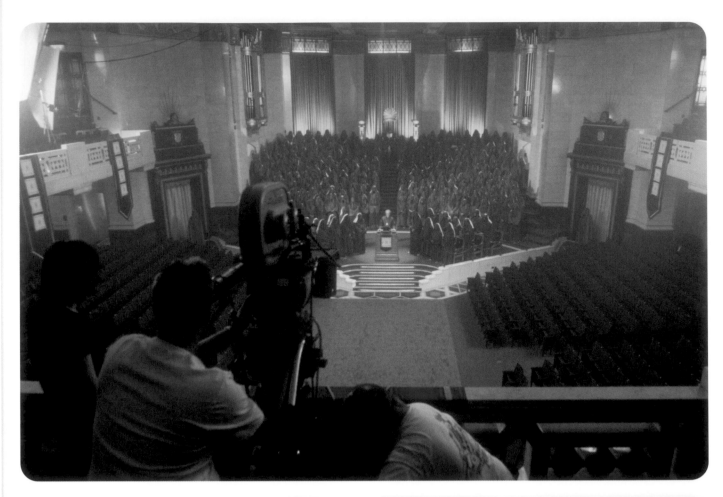

Filming the ranks of devotees

'The extras were dressed in blue and green robes and because it was hot, they went to sit outside during breaks in the filming,' Nick recalls. 'The Freemasons are thought of as this secret society, and some of the general public walking by thought that they were masons in their secret robes. They got harangued by some woman on a bicycle!'

when he takes his glasses off, there are these horrible sunken pits, and when he lifts himself up, there are these amazing legs. If we had made the Temple a freaky place, it would have killed the lovely "reveal" of him getting up and these hundreds of little legs crawling across the table.'

Humma Kavula's temple was filmed at the Freemasons Grand Temple in London. 'There were lots of ideas scouted for that,' location manager David Broder. 'We were trying to avoid a typical church layout, or a conference centre. We looked at the Royal Institute lecture theatre, which is where Douglas Adams gave a couple of lectures, and at some caves in Gibraltar. When we came to look at the Grand Temple, our director of photography Igor saw the size and shape of Humma's quarters, and knew it was right straightaway.'

Humma Kavula
reveals his hidden
sides

'I was surprised that we were allowed to film there, and it's an amazingly film-friendly place,' Nick Goldsmith says. 'There were some areas we shot in that hadn't been shot before. Everyone was really professional – from John Malkovich and the people who ran the Freemasons, down to us.'

Turning the Hall into the Temple wasn't a major job for the production, in terms of decoration at least – 'It was more about filling the Hall with Humma's followers, although we did make some banners and altar cloths incorporating large white handkerchiefs,' Kate Beckly says – but Humma Kavula's office location up numerous flights of stairs caused some logistical problems. The centrepiece of Humma Kavula's office was a table made of gold noses, which had to be carried up manually, since the elevators in the building were too small. 'There was a hell of a lot of work in that table,' construction co-ordinator Steve Bohan says. 'Some of the noses were made of fibreglass, and some from casting plaster – anything to keep the weight down when we were carrying it.'

'The whole of the Arkleseizure Temple is about the nose,' Joel Collins points out. 'The Temple itself is a 40ft stone sculpt of Douglas's nose! There's a frieze entirely made of noses. Creating a table of noses that didn't look stupid was very hard, You look at it and think that it's a nice table, and then realize it's hundreds of noses.'

'Some of the Masons walked in and couldn't believe what we'd been able to do,' Kate adds. 'We had to level out the floor because it was tiered, then built the table and various pedestals around the room, with weird and wonderful treasures from round the galaxy that Humma has collected.'

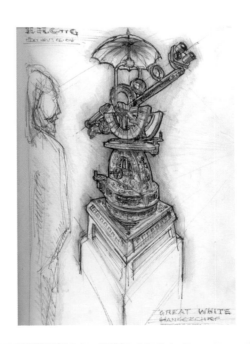

Opposite top: Star Goat design
Opposite bottom left: Incense burner under construction
Opposite bottom right: Humma's handkerchief detector
Below left: Finished Star Goat
Left: Note the sneezing martyrs behind Arthur

SAVE YOUR NOSE

Anita Dhillon created a special logo for Humma Kavula with the Latin inscription *Sternumentum Beoare Munctum* (Sneeze, blow, clean a nose). 'That was turned into a vacform on the front of the Temple,' she notes. 'Normally a graphic designer deals with print, but on Hitchhikers, you'd suddenly see your work as a huge three-dimensional structure.'

THE TEMPLE OF HUMMA KAVULA

'Relentless blighters...'

Slartibartfast, *The Hitchhiker's Guide to the Galaxy*

The Vogon soldiers

The design for the Vogon soldiers was inspired by their first major appearance in the movie, when 'they come out of the fog on Viltvodle with these ridiculous headlights and lit-up mouths,' Garth Jennings recalls. 'Everything has a fixed expression – it's like Hannibal Lecter with his face mask.'

Garth knew that he didn't want to make the soldiers scary 'in a Darth Maul sort of way. Jeltz is rather ridiculous, a big, silly guy like Richard Griffiths's Uncle Monty in *Withnail & I*, but we needed them to pose some kind of threat. The last thing we wanted to do was create stealth Vogons who could leap out and do anything! The rough idea I had was that visually they were like giant avocados, but I couldn't get it right, so I went back to what scared me as a child. I remember seeing a clip of The Elephant Man walking down the street

with a bag over his head, and one eye – and I had nightmares for months after that! The Vogon soldiers would be like zombies: they didn't have horrible guns, but there was something relentless and creepy about them. You could outrun them, but when you stopped and congratulated yourself, there'd be another one there. They just keep going. They don't question. They just do what they're told.'

Because there were often 15 soldiers on screen at a time, 'we had to have a way to cover them because we couldn't afford to have all of them with flesh sticking out. They had rubber suits, and the original design was almost like a hangman's hood, with just the eyeholes cut out. We added some rim lights to the eyes and around the mouth, and made them sufficiently intimidating and odd that no-one's going to want to hang around with them too much!'

The soldiers were cast following an audition at an opera school in Swiss Cottage, north London. 'The audition was

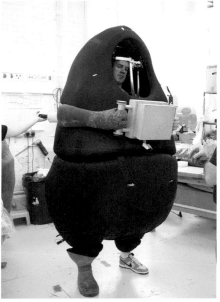

Preparing the Vogon Soldiers at the Jim Henson Creature Shop

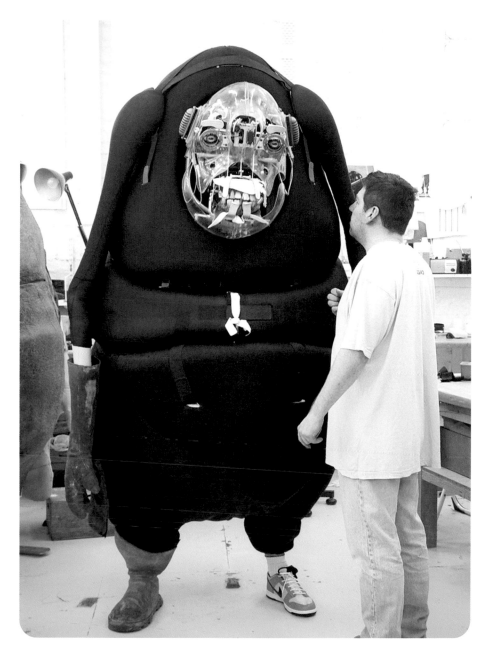

organized by Peter Elliott, who was in charge of all the performance directing,' Creature Shop producer Tracy Lenon explains. 'It was a little bit chicken and egg because when we did the castings, we didn't have suits ready for them to wear, so they had to pretend to be Vogon soldiers.'

Each soldier needed to have his own support team who would get him in and out of the costume, and provide the boxes that they could use to rest on when they weren't filming. Peter Elliott remembers that initially there was a great deal of confusion as the dressers tried to find their own Vogon from the 15 identical '9ft-high baked potatoes' shuffling around, until they allotted each Vogon its own number.

STUBBORN & INFLEXIBLE

Peter Elliott remembers rehearsing the Vogon soldiers march on Viltvodle for the first time in costume, and being very pleasantly surprised and impressed that they were able to shuffle across the room virtually as required. He was rather more alarmed when it took 45 minutes to get them turned around, and brought back to their marks ready for a second rehearsal!

'It was very hot inside the soldier suits, you couldn't get out on your own and there was no light,' Tracy continues. 'They had a little bit of vision through the mouth, and when they weren't facing the cameras, we'd put a little stick in their mouths to give them a little bit more vision. A couple of the high-end animatronic ones had a monitor on the inside so the guys could see their performance, but the others just had earpieces and were effectively blind. They could move their arms inside the suits. When they were sitting on their boxes, they'd have little torches shining down to read a book! Two of them would often play cards, and we'd see these two huge black pods with little feet, and cards being handed over the top!'

In what Jamie Courtier describes as 'the Creature Shopish way', his team made a virtue of necessity. 'We invented these huge bicycle patch repair kits for the soldiers,' he remembers. 'We thought they'd be pretty knocked about, and if they were wearing these great heavy rubber suits, they'd get punctures, so what would they use? We made loads of these patches from 4–12 cm across, and we could use them if they had a puncture. Normally you'd worry about them being seen on camera!'

'Fifteen identical 9ft-high baked potatoes shuffling around...'

Performance director Peter Elliott

The Vogon soldiers line up for battle on location in Hertfordshire

Vogsphere

'Vogons ... wouldn't even lift a finger to save their own grandmothers from the Ravenous Bugblatter Beast of Traal without orders signed in triplicate, sent in, sent back, queried, lost, found, subjected to public inquiry, lost again, and finally buried in soft peat for three months and recycled as fire-lighters.'

The Hitchhiker's Guide to the Galaxy

The Vogons catch up with the Heart of Gold crew, and capture Trillian, believing her to be responsible for the kidnapping of the President. Arthur insists that they go to the Vogons' home world, Vogsphere, to rescue her ...

'*Star Wars™* has the big mythological stuff,' Garth Jennings laughs, 'but our guys have to queue up to rescue someone. Like so many of Douglas's ideas, this is a real spin on something you encounter in everyday life – people at the passport office, or traffic wardens. The trick we found with the Vogons was making them bureaucratic and irritating, but not boring to watch: we were making bureaucracy fun!'

Initially the Heart of Gold crew were simply travelling to Vogsphere to get the necessary permit in order to visit Magrathea. When the kidnapping was added, 'we decided we had to put Arthur in the driving seat,' Garth recalls, meaning the phrase both metaphorically and literally, as he takes the controls of the Heart of Gold's 'Red escape ship which is more like a millionaire's Venetian launch than an escape pod,' as Joel Collins points out.

Above: Warwick Davis on location in the quarry
Left: Artwork and the final design for the marvellously bejwelled Vogon crabs

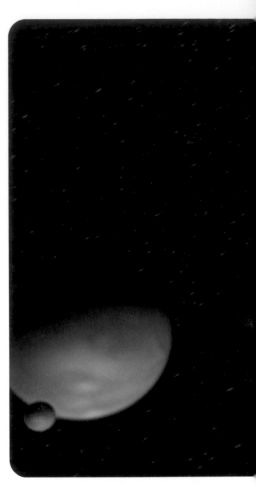

'It's like hiring a flashy car that you have no idea how to use,' Garth continues. 'The first thing you always do in a hire car is indicate right, and set off the wipers instead. I love the stupid little steering wheel that comes out, which is the most ineffectual thing you've ever seen.'

'We built a full-size model in polystyrene,' Asylum's Mark Mason explains. 'That was then laminated over in fibreglass, and laboriously rubbed down to get it smooth. Then it was primed with a hardened filler, primer and paint which was then baked hard in an oven.'

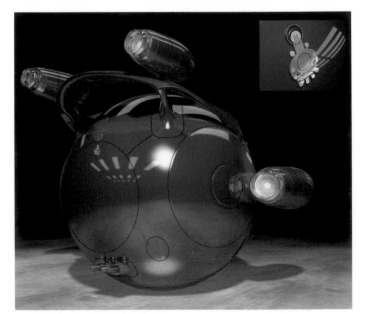

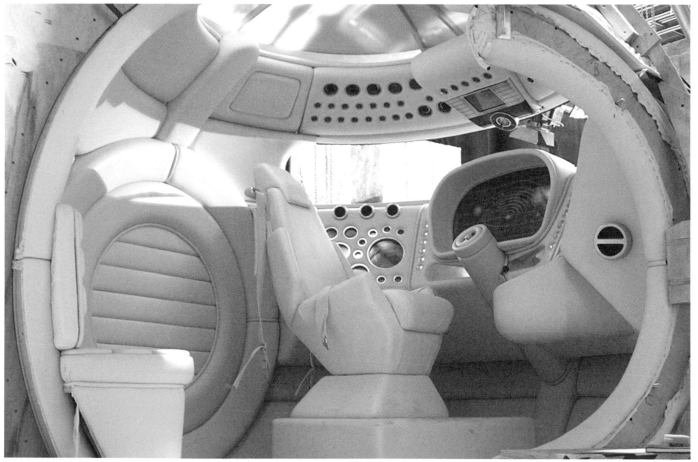

HEY, I KNOW ... THWACK

Although most of the paddles that come up and smack the characters in the face whenever they have an idea were added in post-production, the cast still had to run across the quarry so they could be composited into the scene. On this occasion, Nick and Garth's assistant Lita Bleichman donned a lightweight version of the Marvin suit (right).

out great. The weather was up and down, but it was brilliant – we were on top of a Welsh mountain, in a quarry with helicopters and a crashed spaceship!'

'It was lovely to walk round in those miserable conditions, with all the grey rock, and see this bright red spaceship sitting there,' Mark Mason notes. 'And when it was in the pit with the flames burning behind it, it was quite an impressive sight!'

Everyone's overwhelming memory of the location in Wales was that it was cold. 'But there was Warwick in the huge Marvin suit almost three-quarters of his body weight, who never fumbled once, never complained or demanded to be put in the carriage,' Garth recalls. 'He was out there in the middle of a rainstorm with thunder and lightning coming down, with the wind whistling up the gaps in his little rubber suit.'

Although he believes he almost got hypothermia, despite the large number of layers of clothing he was wearing, Sam Rockwell remembers that the scene with the paddles 'really comes down to being a kid and playing cops and robbers, or cowboys and Indians. That sequence in particular is about the bare, essential, childlike state that you're in when you're acting. Mos, Martin and I were five or ten years old, just pretending that there were wooden paddles rising up from the ground and hitting us in the face.'

During the initial location scout, Garth and Nick had visited Iceland. 'We were looking at these volcanic beds that just go on for about 50 miles on the west coast,' Garth says. 'It would have been perfect for the Vogons, with this green bulging flat land that went straight out to sea, but so expensive for us to film it was ludicrous. Also, ecologically, we would have really screwed the place up. The moss was 1,000 years old, and the minute you stood on it, that bit died – imagine a camera crew there! So we decided to film it in Britain, and I told the location managers not to choose a quarry because of the associations with all those 'alien planets' in *Doctor Who* that were really quarries.'

However Vogsphere *was* shot in a quarry in Wales. 'They did a really smart job,' Garth admits. 'They showed me these photographs which were all misty, and told me it was in Wales. The photos were brilliant, and only then did they tell me it was a quarry! It was a trek to get up there, but it worked

'...huge chunky yellow slablike somethings, huge as office blocks, silent as birds...'

The Hitchhiker's Guide to the Galaxy

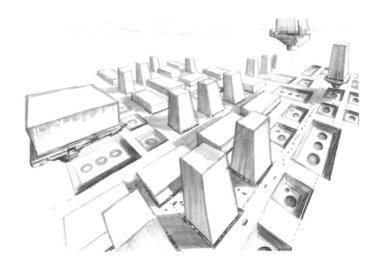

Vogcity

'There's no logic to some science-fiction cities,' Joel Collins notes. 'You don't feel that you're in a specific space – you're in some weird, non-tangible space. We wanted to make it so that everywhere Arthur goes outside the sanctuary of the Heart of Gold is a bit bleak and scary. It's not too "in-your-face" with monsters coming out of every crevice, just unsettling to a human.'

Rather than have some fancy spaceport where the huge Vogon ships could come into land, Joel argued – since one of the main reasons that the Vogons returned home would be to recharge their ships with the necessary supplies – why not take that one stage further and actually have them land on a three-pin plug? Everything has to make sense, so why not use a plug? 'We took an ordinary plug, and built it as if it was 200ft high. The Vogon ships land and charge up – and all of them together make a concrete jungle.'

The Vogon ships weren't created in computer graphics. 'Our gut instinct was to make them with miniatures even though the scale was a challenge,' visual effects supervisor Angus Bickerton explains. 'At 1/500th scale, a 1 mile-high tower block translates to about 10ft tall. Once you put that on 2ft-high decks in the studio, and get your camera right down to scale eye height, which is millimetres off the floor, you're suddenly looking up into the top of the studio. You can see the rigs and the gantries.' Getting the textures

correct at such a small scale was also a problem. 'The doorway was about 8mm tall at best.'

One of the first guidelines for the film that Garth passed to the visual effects crew was that he preferred the texture of the effects work in the original version of *Star Wars: The Empire Strikes Back* to that of *The Phantom Menace*. 'In those first films, it was all done with miniatures, not done with CGI as the Special Editions and the new films are,' Angus says. 'That led to us using miniatures for this movie, because we knew we would get the textures right. Directors constantly say they want organic textures, because they feel sensitive to the difference between them and computer graphics. Surprisingly enough, the cost wasn't that much different – it was cheaper doing models ultimately, but the man hours do start to equate between 10 people in a workshop and one or two people at a computer.'

Above: Artwork for VogCity
Opposite middle: Vogon bus designs
Opposite bottom left: Vogon bus poster ('This Could Be You!')
Opposite bottom right: Shooting the miniature of VogCity

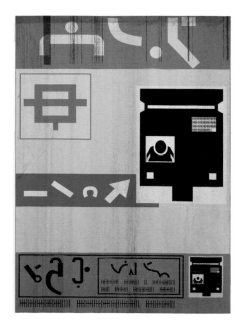

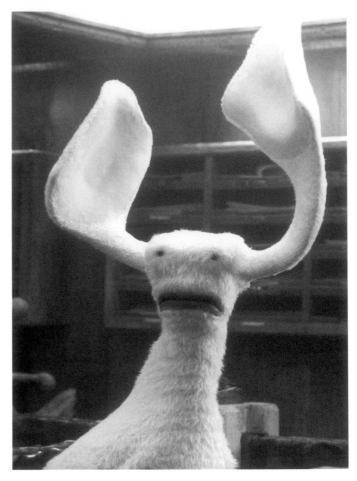

The room in which the Heart of Gold crew queue up in order to get the necessary paperwork stamped to save Trillian was a revamped version of another Vogon set, populated by a large number of alien races all caught up in the bureaucracy. Many of these were created by the Wimbledon Art College students, while some of the favourites from the Viltvodle sequence made a reappearance. Kate Beckly and Anita Dhillon worked together again to create a viable environment for the Vogon paper pushers, with oversize biros attached to ridiculously short pieces of chain, and each of the Vogon forms specifically created for whatever the occurrence.

Puppeteer Mak Wilson was quite surprised when he realized that Sam Rockwell and Martin Freeman were improvising on the set since it wasn't simply a question of one person having to react to what they said – the whole

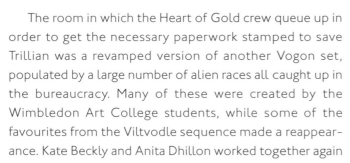

Top left: A Vogon stapler
Above right: Fynn.
Opposite: The Mexican Jumping Bean

puppeteering team had to work in unison to provide a response. 'There was all this banter, and Garth hadn't told us that we were going to be improvising,' he recalls. 'They suddenly went off the script, and we had to play along with it – and doing that with animatronics is always a challenge! It's always wonderful when you get four people come together to make a character. You just merge and make a living thing.'

ALL DOWN MY LEFT SIDE

Also waiting patiently is a tall metal creature that was instantly familiar to fans of the previous screen incarnation of Hitchhikers. The Marvin robot from the 1981 television edition made a special guest cameo. The twenty-three-year-old costume was refurbished from the waist up for the moment when two generations of Marvin met.

Opposite top right:
Classic and New
Marvin meet
Above: Artwork
showing the pod's
escape from VogCity
Right and below:
Questular and the
Vogons watch the Pod
depart

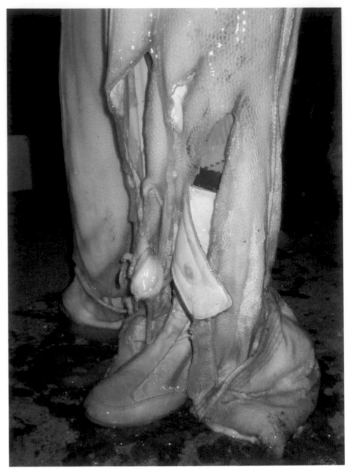

Trillian is interrogated, chained up, and fed to the Ravenous Bug Blatter Beast of Traal

'... such a mind-boggingly stupid animal it assumes that if you can't see it, it can't see you ...'

The Hitchhiker's Guide to the Galaxy

The Ravenous Bug Blatter Beast of Traal

One of Asylum's biggest props was the box inside which the Ravenous Bug Blatter Beast of Traal is waiting to eat Trillian. 'It was quite nice for us to start the shoot on something that was nice and big,' Mark Mason comments. 'It wasn't as complicated as it looked, but it was a 14 x 10 x 10ft box that had to move very quickly.'

To make the box move as necessary, Asylum created a control box which the operator could hold in his hand, and whatever was done to the one being held was replicated by the larger box. 'The challenge was keeping it safe all the time,' Mark says. 'The prop weighed just over a ton, and we had to keep it moving fast but still keep Zooey safe as she was hanging over it.'

Tons of alien slime were created for the Bugblatter Beast to drool everywhere. 'The Beast was salivating to such a point that the crew had to wear paper overalls because of the tons of slime that was being catapulted out of the box as it was working. It was actually funnier inside the box than outside!'

Zooey Deschanel wasn't nervous at performing the stunt herself, and hanging dozens of feet above the studio floor. 'I used to rock climb when I was a kid so I was pretty used to harnesses,' she points out. 'I know how safe they are. I figured it was best to do it myself because you have more control that way. Every once in a while they have to use a stunt double, but it's better to do a stunt yourself if you can. There was a lot of physical acting involved but I wanted to have control over it.'

'It is important to note that suddenly, and against all probability, a sperm whale had been called into existence several miles above the surface of an alien planet. And since this is not a naturally tenable position for a whale, this innocent creature had very little time to come to terms with its identity as a whale before it then had to come to terms with suddenly not being a whale any more.'

The Hitchhiker's Guide to the Galaxy

The Whale

The reunited crew argue about using the IID to get them to Magrathea, but the Drive is triggered by Trillian's two mice who have been observing the crew's actions. An ancient defence system fires two missiles at them, but Arthur saves the day by hitting the IID button again, turning the missiles into a rather surprised-looking sperm whale and a bunch of petunias …

The Creature Shop's Verner Gresty was responsible for building a whale that would both look natural, but also be able to do what was required of it in the script.

From early discussions with Garth and Angus, it was decided that the whale had to be as realistic as possible. With this in mind, a sculptor with particular experience in natural history projects was engaged, and as much reference as possible was assembled. This included several video tapes to judge the movement of sperm whales, as well as their form.

A scale was chosen to enable enough detail to be incorporated into the sculpt for close-up camera work, while not making the model so large as to be a problem on set. Eventually a length of just over 10ft was chosen. From the

outset the whale was to be mounted upside down on a slim pole arm or boom to enable it to be raised off the floor by some 10 to 12ft so the camera would be free to 'roam' around the model at will. It was upside down so that water droplets sprayed on the skin would move *up* the body as the whale falls through the clouds.

The scene did not require the whale to talk, but his eyes had to be very expressive and able to take a close-up. The tail needed to have a wide range of movement as did the flippers, and the body would have a small amount of side-to-side movement. The pole arm itself entered the body roughly half-way along, and enabled the whale to roll and pitch about the centre of gravity.

Once the overall size was decided, outline drawings were made and scaled up. A strong metal armature was welded together and mounted on a moveable base. This was then covered in chicken wire and plaster, and finally in clay to allow the finished whale to be moulded. A fibreglass mould was applied and then removed so that the clay could be cleaned out, and a fresh layer laid inside. More fibreglass was moulded to the inside of this clay.

The clay was removed, leaving a space in the fibreglass 'sandwich' which could be injected with the material to make the skin of the whale. As the shoot would involve the model being sprayed with water and a very realistic fleshy

movement was needed, the skin was made out of solid Urethane rubber — this meant the skin weighed some 140 kg. The flippers were moved by large radio-controlled motors, and the eyes and eyelids were powered by smaller versions.

The larger body movements were achieved by using pneumatic rams inside the body linked to larger rams by some 40ft of hoses and connections to lever controls. So as to get a direct controlled movement the system was filled with water.

At the end of the 17-week building process, the final finishing detail was applied with coarse sand being used to imitate scale barnacles.

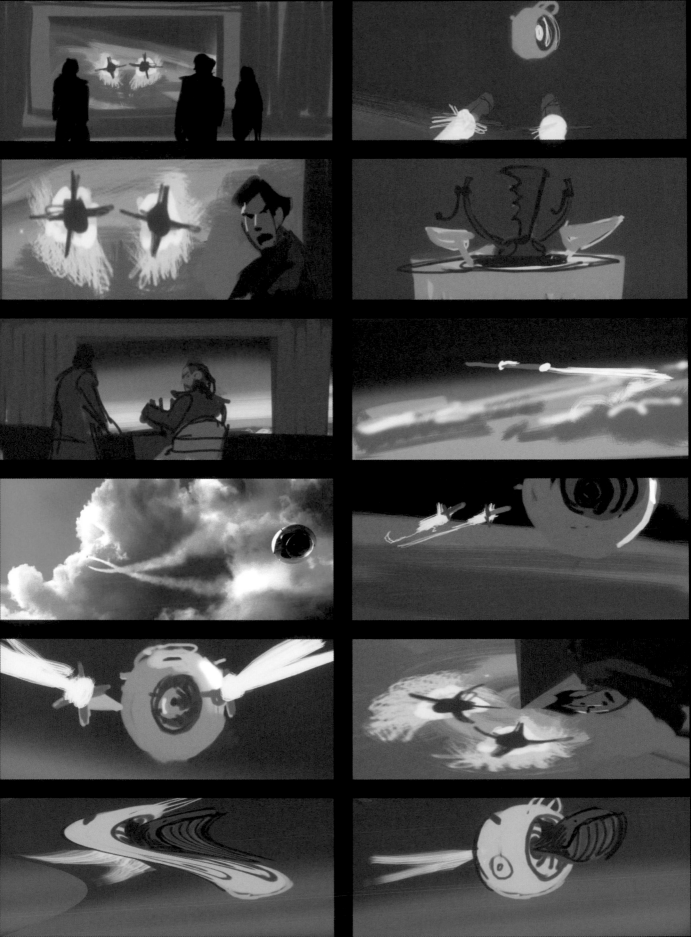

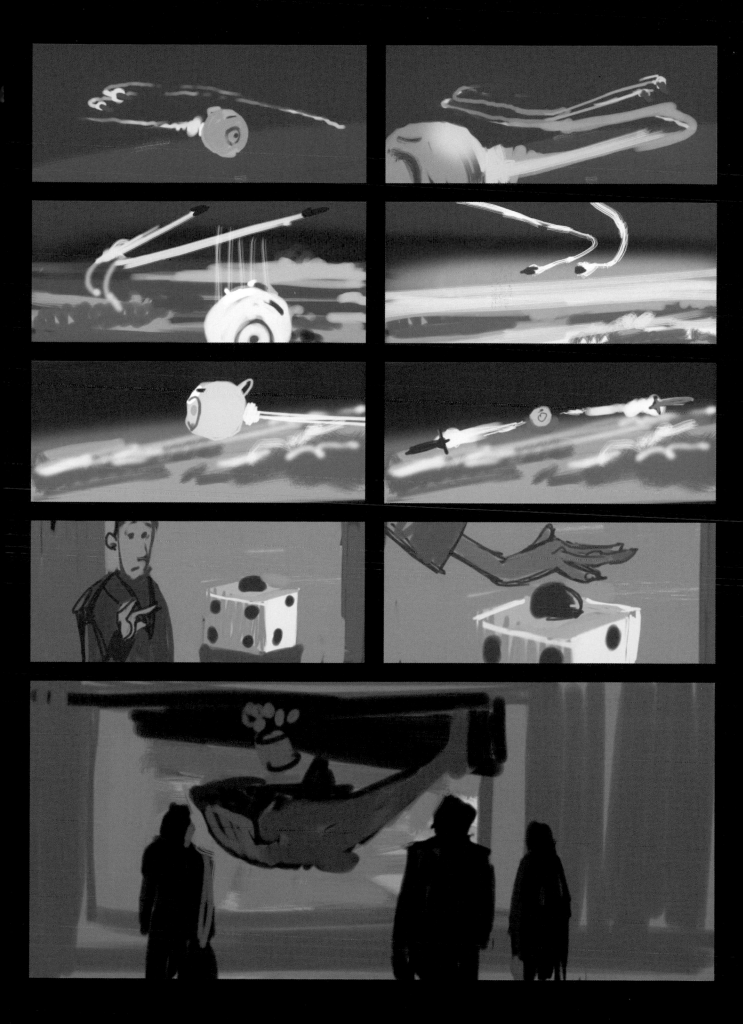

LITTLE WHITE FURRY THINGS

Second Unit director Dominic Leung was in charge of filming the sequences with the mice. 'We did some camera tests before we started which were quite positive,' he explains. 'We used macro lenses in order to be able to get a mouse face filling up a third of the film, and shot them at high speed as well, because they're so twitchy. We could slow them down and they still would look natural with a more talkative expression. That worked in very short bursts. We would get a second in real time which translated to four seconds in the end.'

Dominic expected that what they referred to as 'the A to B stuff' – scenes where the mice run around the Heart of Gold – would be easy enough to film. 'That turned out to be a complete and utter nightmare,' he admits. 'You'd think there would be some magical trick to get them to do it, like leaving female mouse urine as a trail, but it simply came from repetition. If you want the mouse to run from left to right along a wall, you put it down near the wall. It'll probably run forward a little bit and come away from the wall, so you put it back at the beginning, and do it again. It's the most monotonous thing you can think of, but it's just repetition. It will do it eventually when it realizes that when you leave it alone, it's doing the right thing, and when it's not, you put it back to the beginning so it's getting nowhere.

'We couldn't go away and leave them,' he adds. 'It was like watching paint dry sometimes. As soon as we stepped away for a break, they'd do it! We had to devise other ways of making it simpler. When we wanted the mice together, we shot them separately, and locked off the camera so that we could combine the shots. But they started to get better, and when we were doing the scene on the console, they started to get it right.'

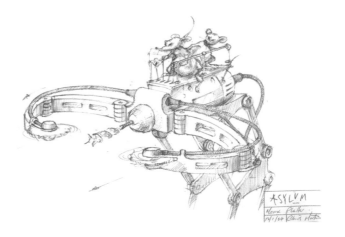

Above: Concept design and finished prop for the mice's brain retriever
Below: The stunt mice

Opposite: Franky and Benjy Mouse ponder The Question

THE MAKING OF **THE HITCHHIKER'S GUIDE TO THE GALAXY**

ZZ 9 PLURAL Z ALPHA

The team were always very aware that they were adding to the Hitchhiker canon and wanted to be respectful of what had gone before. Casting Simon Jones, the original Arthur Dent in both the radio and TV series, was the best example of just that. 'We were very keen to find a small role for Simon,' Robbie Stamp says, 'and although the original thought was that he could play the barman who serves Ford and Arthur at the start of the film, playing the ghostly image who warns the team off Magrathea was perfect. Simon came to the bluescreen studios at Shepperton towards the very end of the shoot. We had decided to shoot this scene in 3D so just in case anybody sneaks into the cinema with the right glasses they will see a disembodied three-dimensional head in space. We were all really happy to have his face and voice in the movie.'

'Thus were created the conditions for a staggering new form of specialist industry: custom-made luxury planet building. The home of this industry was the planet Magrathea, where hyperspatial engineers sucked matter through white holes in space to form it into dream planets...'

The Guide, Page 634784, Section 5a, *The Hitchhiker's Guide to the Galaxy*

Magrathea

Landing on Magrathea, Ford, Zaphod and Trillian go through one portal to the home of Deep Thought, looking for the location of the Ultimate Computer and the Point of View Gun, while Arthur meets Slartibartfast, one of the last Magratheans, who gives him a guided tour of the planet factory floor and their new project — Earth II ...

Top: Artwork for Magrathea
Above: Background added by Cinesite
Opposite: Location scouting in Iceland
Below: Warwick Davis and Garth on the studio set at Shepperton

The main reason that Iceland was scouted for Hitchhikers was to provide a potential location to shoot the glacier-bound scenes on the surface of Magrathea. 'That was doable,' producer Todd Arnow recalls, 'but when we evaluated the entire plan, we realized that creating a snowy environment on a sound stage was much more controllable, and it would give Garth more time to get the performance out of the actors. In Iceland, the weather and the light

available at the time of year we'd be there would limit us creatively.'

'We found this amazing glacier,' Garth adds. 'It was really extraordinary, but if we were shooting in the summer, the tourists would be there and the snow would go black.'

The scenes were finally shot at Shepperton Studios, which became the home for all the bluescreen work that was needed for the movie, particularly the extended sequence in which Slartibartfast shows Arthur around the planet factory floor.

JUST LIKE THAT

The Deep Thought sequences demonstrated special effects tricks that span the entire history of cinema. Deep Thought itself was a miniature, some of the environment around was matted into the picture using computer graphics, and Zaphod's arrival 'is the oldest cinema trick in history,' according to Angus Bickerton. 'It was probably the first gag that cinema pioneer Georges Méliès ever did – a straight jump-cut. You throw in a dummy, stop the camera, the actor goes in and lines himself up in the same position, and then start the camera up again. We're supposed to be as cutting-edge and as up-to-date as possible, but it's a funny gag, and it still works.'

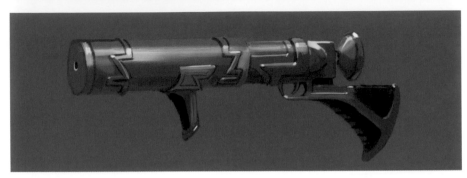

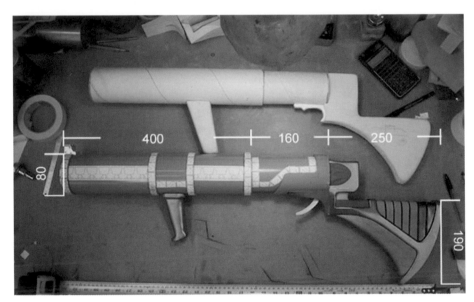

The Point of View Gun

The Point of View gun was one of the major conceptual additions to the Hitchhikers myth that Douglas Adams created during the long process of bringing the story to the big screen. With the emphasis of the screenplay focusing on Arthur and Trillian's relationship, it was a 'fantastic way to handle a major inflection point in the movie without Trillian having to perform a soliloquy. Douglas was always very wary of sentiment, and this is a very clever Hitchhikery way to handle a big emotional moment,' Robbie Stamp points out. For Garth Jennings, 'sitting on the bottom of the cameras, and watching Zooey respond to Sam as Trillian's feelings were unravelled in front of her was brilliant.'

'We went through a load of designs for the gun,' Joel Collins says. 'We didn't want to make guns that looked dangerous, since it's a Disney film. And it's not a gun like an M16 that's going to be used to slaughter everyone. It has a very different process. When you look at the gun, you see an old-style flashbulb which has a mirror in it, facing back at your body. That in turn flashes and that flash absorbs your personality, then punches it through a lens at the front onto the person you're shooting. If you want to shoot at a mass, then it works like a telescope: you flip open the front and the lens gets a lot bigger.'

The design reflects elements of Deep Thought's own appearance. 'Deep Thought is covered in gold, and has the emblem of his head everywhere,' Joel adds, 'so obviously on the gun that's used by his protectors, his emblem is on it.'

'Douglas was always very wary of sentiment, and this is a very clever Hitchhikery way to handle a big emotional moment.'

Executive producer Robbie Stamp

Slartibartfast

'The first person we ever thought of for the cast was Bill Nighy,' Garth Jennings says. 'We had all just seen him in the TV series *State of Play*, and he took all the jargon that he had to say and made it sound interesting and funny. It's easy to say "I love you", and that emotional stuff, but to say "We need to get the papers to stop the print run – and get that guy on the phone" in such a pizzazzy way is much, much harder. We knew he'd be able to do Slartibartfast. Just give him a bit of hair and a big coat!'

'He needed to look otherworldly,' costume designer Sammy Sheldon notes, 'But at the same time he's an artist who builds planets. The whole shape of what he's wearing came from an artist's smock. It's made from pure silk – Garth saw a roll of it and fell in love with it. When it's raw and unwashed, it's all knobbly. Underneath he's got almost-Armani style linen trousers, and a shirt with a nice silk tie, all in beige. There's a link to a sort of "God" look, but keeping it very modern.'

Right and below: designs for various graphics and displays from the Showroom

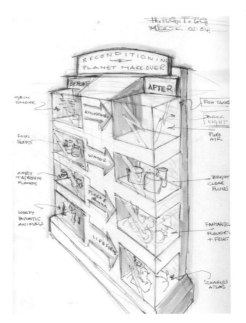

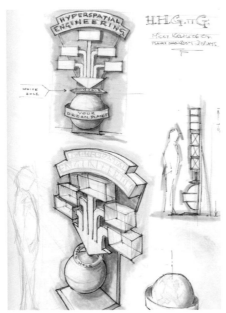

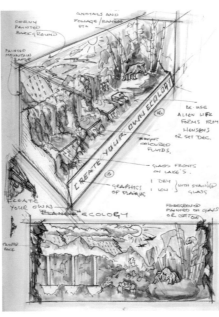

WE ALSO STOCK OFF THE PEG COASTLINE MOULDINGS STENCILS, WHICH CAN BE ADAPTED TO YOUR NEEDS

SHAPE YOUR LANDMASS WITH OUR *AWARD WINNING COASTLINES*

MODERATE ECOSYSTEM

SIMPLE/CALM ECOSYSTEM

DRAMATIC ECOSYSTEM

SHAPELY COASTLINES IMPROVE THE BEAUTY OF YOUR PLANET

SPECIAL METHODS ENABLE ANY COMPLICATED SHAPE TO BE TRACED AND MADE INTO A COASTLINE *

WHY NOT LET US TRACE ONE OF YOUR BEST FEATURES INTO A COASTLINE?
*SHAPE IS DEPENDENT ON WEATHER SYSTEM OF YOUR PLANET

AWARDED TO THOSE WHO POSSESS THE FINEST SKILLS TO DESIGN THE MOST EXQUISITE COASTLINERY THAT MAY ENRICH, COLOUR, EMBELLISH AND PROVIDE LOVELY SUNBATHING LOCATIONS FOR THE PLANET'S PATRONS   IGG

THE PLANET SHOWROOM

The factory elements were also built at Shepperton, with numerous graphic additions by Anita Dhillon. 'We were making up stupid names for planets, and writing absolute rubbish,' she laughs, 'My brain just went into a different zone while I was doing that, and stuff would just come out. You didn't have time to think about things in any sort of detail, just create and create.'

HGG - PLANET FACTORY
VEGAS PLANET I

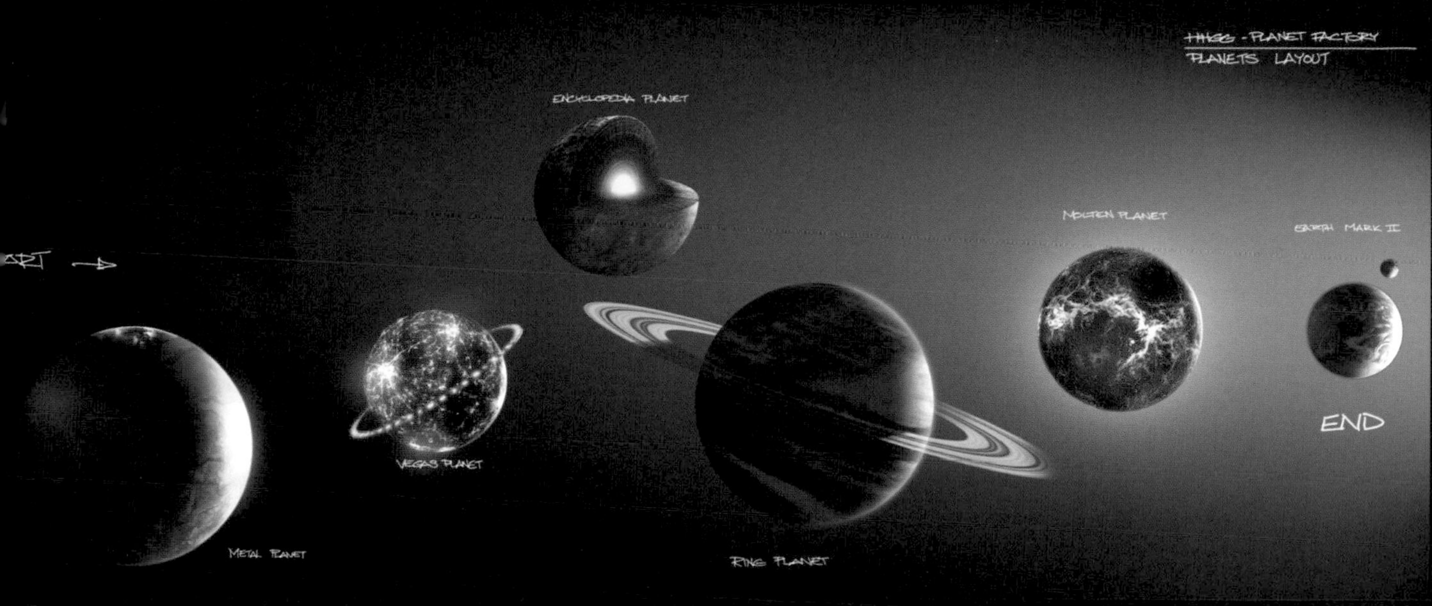

ENCYCLOPEDIA PLANET

MOLTEN PLANET

EARTH MARK II

VEGAS PLANET

RING PLANET

METAL PLANET

END

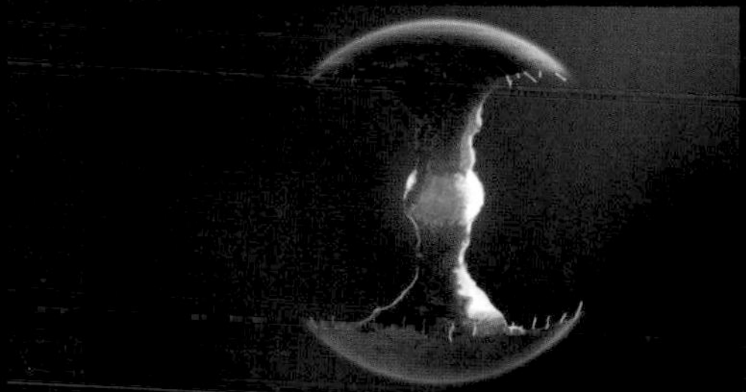

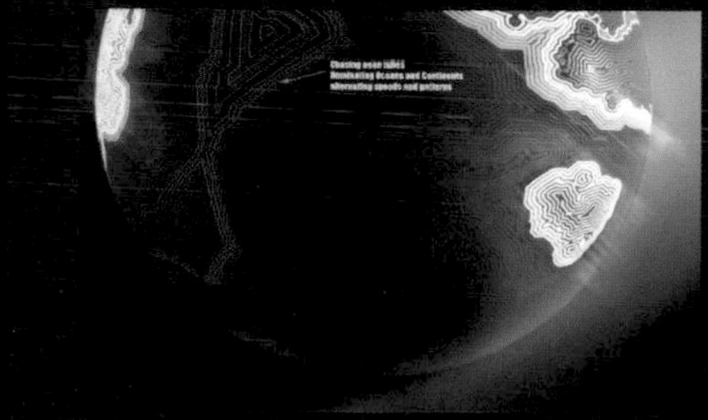

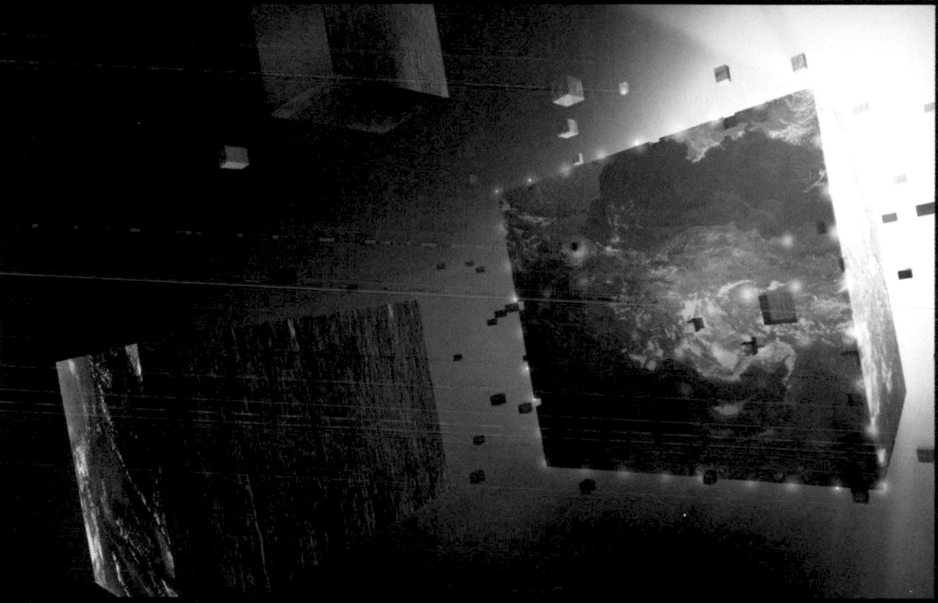

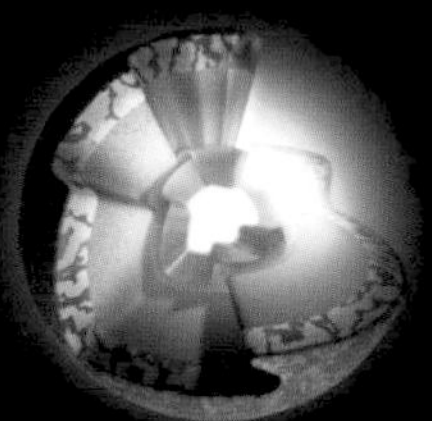

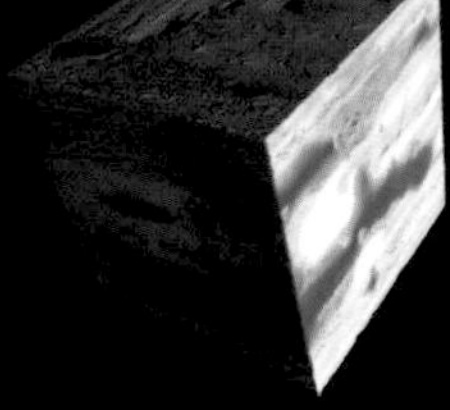

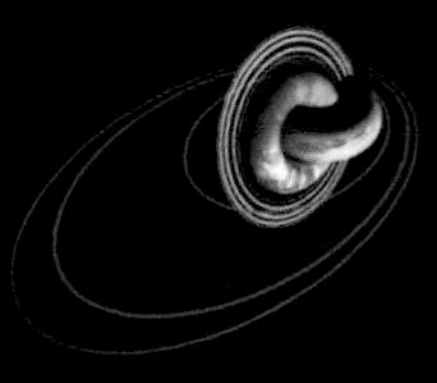

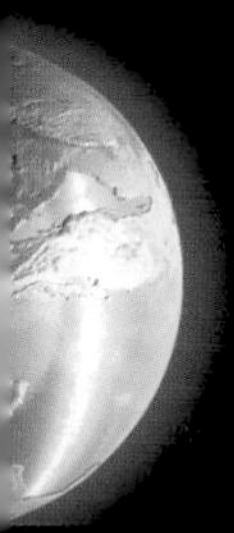

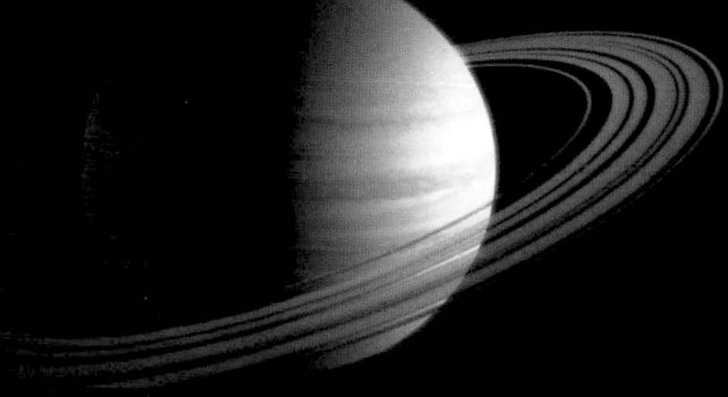

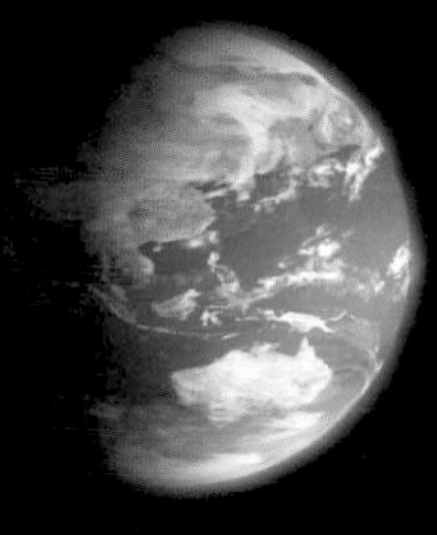

'The chamber into which the aircar emerged was anything but infinite, it was just very very very big, so big that it gave the impression of infinity far better than infinity itself.'

The Hitchhiker's Guide to the Galaxy

The Planet Factory

The Magrathea Planet Factory floor was one of the biggest sequences in all senses that Cinesite had to create. 'That was a long time coming together in pre-viz because of the scope of it,' Joel Collins admits. 'It was a year and a half of design finding the scale and getting it right. It was a real pain – where do you start? The scope is endless. To try to build a planet in a room that's real scale would mean that the room has to be so big that you'll never see the end of the wall, let alone build 30 planets. It's mindnumbing just trying to get your head around the concepts involved. Dan May, who worked with me, conceptualized most of the elements in the computer and then passed them through to Cinesite. Angus Bickerton was involved from early on, because he was the one who was going to have to bring it through during post-

production, and he understands the spatial achievements in computers.'

The role of Cinesite was to turn the ideas that Joel and his team came up with into reality. 'They're a big machine who need information to process,' Joel explains. 'Angus is extremely creative and we were constantly raising the bar for him. We put a lot of work into the Planet Factory elements to make them real. Angus was definitely an advocate of the Art Department having an input into post-production rather than leaving it in their hands. We used all our tools to feed him information which made his job more interesting.'

The sequence was constantly changed throughout the post-production period. 'We will never be critical or argue against something which works better for the film,' Angus says, 'and for the sake of the story, some of the sequence has been cut back.'

Opposite: The deceptively simple aircart in which Slartibartfast and Arthur travel
Left and below: Inside the Planet Factory

Various live action elements are composited into the sequence, based around Bill Nighy and Martin Freeman in the cart. 'That was one of my favourite bits of the film,' Asylum's Mark Mason says. 'Garth's brief was that it would be like an old ghost train with the carts running on air-cushions, so they would behave like a hovercraft. You would lose all friction, so they could corner at high speed and just slip around the central pivot.'

Artwork for the factory workers and their tools

Earth II

'You're trying to tell me that 'mice' ... designed and built Deep Thought ... and Deep Thought designed the Earth ... which was a giant supercomputer ... that you lot built ... to calculate the Ultimate Question. Only, Vogons destroyed it ten minutes before the program was completed?'

Arthur Dent, *The Hitchhiker's Guide to the Galaxy*

Home sweet home?

Arthur's house

Slartibartfast explains that the mice commissioned the ultimate computer, and takes him to the duplicate of his own home on Earth II, where the others are waiting for him. However Fook and Lunkwill, in their guise as Frankie and Benjy Mouse, try to seize Arthur's brain ...

For the scenes set in Arthur's house on Earth II, the production team decided not to film inside the house in Hertfordshire, although the original opening of the film, which featured Arthur waking up and realizing that the bulldozers are outside his windows, was filmed there. 'We recreated the inside of the house back in the studio,' construction co-ordinator Steve Bohan explains. 'Some of the interiors of the house were hard

to light, and of course you can take out a wall if you need to when you're in the studio.'

The duplication wasn't exact, because the dimensions of the dining room were larger. 'And remember, it had just been freshly built by the Magratheans,' Kate Beckly notes, 'so the props and dressing was identical to Arthur's house at the beginning of the film, but this time everything was brand new! We were able to fill it with the feast and the cakes. If we had done that with the house on location, we wouldn't have been able to get the cameras in.'

So much of the film had been planned over pots of tea shared by Garth and members of the production personnel, that it was very appropriate that the penultimate scenes of the movie took place over a feast of tea and cakes. Kate Beckly and her team had fun preparing the repast. 'Arthur had spent the whole film dying for a cup of tea, so we were imagining what each of the characters would be dying for,' she says. 'We

Opposite: Arthur
fights against the
proposed brain
surgery
Below: Two unwanted
guests

wanted unfeasibly high piles of cakes, trifles, sandwiches, fruit, jellies, éclairs, scones and huge chicken drumsticks. There was also the practical point that it was a five-day shoot, so we asked the actors what they would be happy eating over and over again. Our home economist Christine was out the back of the studio making whatever replacements we needed.' While Mos and Zooey ate grapes and strawberries, Sam Rockwell threw caution to the wind and devoured cream cakes because that was exactly what he thought Zaphod would do!

Although they had made brief appearances earlier in the film, extracting a hair from Arthur's head to check his DNA, and activating the Infinite Improbability Drive to get to Magrathea, this was the first time that Frankie and Benjy Mouse had taken centre stage. 'Our mouseman David was a genius,' Kate says in awe. 'The moment I read the script and realized we were going to have the real mice and all that

food in the same scene, I thought we were in for problems, because the way you normally train animals is by using food to entice them to do what you want. I was worried the mice would run off and bury themselves in a cream cake, but full credit to the mouse wrangler. We were able to get great performances out of these mice.'

'By the time we got to the tea party, they were the best trained mice in the world,' Dominic Leung agrees. 'It was quite unbelievable. We were going to use computer-generated mice for the close-ups, and just use the real animals in wide shots, but they just seemed to do what we needed them to do. We'd put them where we wanted them, and after they'd calmed down and got a bit sleepy under the hot lights, we could get them to look to the camera by chewing a bit of chocolate, and blowing breath down a straw at their face to get their attention. We shot a lot of film, but we got it all.'

NOW YOU SEE IT...

Not every special effect is immediately obvious when you watch a movie. Sometimes what viewers don't see is as important as what they do see. 'In some of the film of the mice, you can actually see the crew reflected in the silver spoons on the table,' Angus Bickerton comments. 'When you scan the film images and they're brought up at high resolution on the screen, suddenly you can see the cameraman. We then paint those reflections out on the computer.'

One of the more unusual considerations that had to be factored into the Creature Shop's plans was the high amount of washing generated each day by the Vogon soldiers. 'There were at least 15 T-shirts, socks, shorts and 30–40 towels to wash every day,' Tracy Lenon points out. 'I was staying in a bed and breakfast so couldn't take it home as I had been doing when we were at the studio. I ended up leaving it to one of the security guards to do. It was like dealing with a rugby team, and of course some guys walked around in the mud and expected their clothes somehow to be clean magically in the morning!'

Onward Vogon Soldiers, going as to war!

The Battle for Earth

Arthur saves himself, killing the mice in the process, but the Vogons have arrived. Marvin is caught in the crossfire but still manages to save the day ...

'The battle sequence at the end was one of the biggest location moments,' Robbie Stamp says. 'We had Vogons, all the main cast and an actor who's about to have a little explosion in the back of his head!'

The final confrontation between the Vogons and the Heart of Gold crew was originally scripted to take place on Magrathea. 'The end of the movie was a huge thing with battledroids, and Ford doing *Matrix*-style moves with his towel,' Garth recalls. 'We had a meeting with Karey to try

to find a way to make the battle happen on Arthur's home turf. A big battle scene with physical ingenuity winning the day wasn't really in the spirit of Hitchhikers, and it was at that moment that we decided to give the Point of View gun to Marvin. It had been used earlier between Ford and Zaphod, but then forgotten about. We shot Marvin, and got him out of the picture, which of course no-one would be expecting, and then he turns round and "makes their day".

Originally all the Vogons were so depressed that they shot themselves in the head. I was really excited about them committing suicide, but we realised we might have problems getting that past the censors without being given an 18 certificate because of all the Vogon brains everywhere. I'm really pleased that they just give up and lie down in typical Hitchhikers style.'

QUICK, ITS SPITTING

As well as the ruined debris of Arthur's house, the construction crew also built a copy of the Vogon Constructor Bridge set up in a rather smelly barn at the Hertfordshire location to be used for wet weather cover. 'Everything was about contingencies,' Nick Goldsmith explains. 'If we had light rain and we couldn't shoot outside, what should we do? We could wait for it to pass. Or we could shoot the Vogons on the Constructor Bridge set, or even shoot the scene in the pub which was nearby. But if it was really bad, we would cut our losses and go back to Elstree. We lived out there for two weeks and didn't use the Bridge set, and the Second Unit ended up doing those scenes.'

That had a knock-on effect for the Creature Shop crew, who had to be ready to shoot at a moment's notice. 'We'd unpack everything and be ready to go, but not end up doing anything,' Tracy Lenon says. 'Then we'd have to go back to Elstree because they were shooting something with the soldiers down there.'

AWESOME FIREPOWER

'The Vogon guns were rusty old metal like all bits of machinery are,' Asylum's Mark Mason says. 'They were nine-barrel weapons, which would appear to be randomly firing. However each gun was programmed differently. They all fired at the same speed, but no two sequences were the same. Carbon dioxide (CO_2) was fired through a bank of electronic displays which would only light up when the CO_2 was released. We had electronics on board to control the CO_2 valves and the lighting, and we made backpacks for the Vogons which contained the CO_2 and the batteries to power them.'

'When I read that scene in the script, I wondered what kind of comedy I could draw from it,' Marvin actor Warwick Davis says. 'But Garth wanted it played for the emotion of the moment. He shot it in slow motion. It was quite challenging – I was the one releasing the four squibs in the head, as well as staggering backwards and forwards, rotating round and making sure that I didn't fall over. When they put the big crater in the back of the head, it made it quite a few pounds heavier than it already was, so the balance was off as well. But we managed to get it in one take, and I didn't fall over until I was meant to!'

Warwick deservedly received a round of applause at the end of the take from cast and crew, and was then taken out of the costume. 'We laid the empty costume on the ground,' his dresser Paul Jomain remembers, 'and after two or three hours, one of the sparks came up to me and asked if Warwick was OK, or if he needed a break!'

Once the scenes with the main cast had been filmed, the Second Unit took over to shoot the Vogons' side of the battle. 'We were always just waiting for the right cloud to match what the main unit had shot,' Dominic Leung notes. 'We were at the mercy of the weather. We were outside and it was quite hot and with the heads on the Vogons could last about the length of a roll of film. The problem was that the gas canisters that shot the CO_2 out of the guns only lasted a couple of minutes. Every time we set something up, the odds were stacked against us and time was slipping away. We were chasing the light right to the end of the day. But we got it all, and we got it good.'

Earth II boots up

The final sequence of the movie, as Earth II is triggered, very consciously mirrors earlier sections set on Earth during the film. 'Instead of a montage of gratuitous stock footage, we go backwards and see lightning strike the ground, the fish in the sea, the oceans now filled up,' Garth says. 'Even Douglas's mum will be back in the cafe reading the newspaper as she was at the start.'

Magrathean Planet Workers tidy up after the Vogons

The Legacy

For many seasoned professionals, the movie has been an unusually pleasant experience. For Executive producer Robbie Stamp, the whole period – from thinking about the movie, to the web, the games, the mobile tie-ins, and the DVD – has been an exercise in love and respect for Douglas. 'All along we have tried to make something which those who already know Hitchhikers in its other incarnations will love, and which all those who haven't yet experienced the invention, intelligence and humour that lie at the heart of Douglas's genius will come to love,' he comments.

'It has been a movie of singular vision,' Karey Kirkpatrick says. 'There was no movie-making by a committee of writers. The core team was very small and I think it shows. We did need to amend and create stuff, but the goal was always to go to something very Douglassy. That inspired the creation, so everything felt like it belonged in the universe that he created. Because Douglas had died and there was this

overwhelming feeling that we wanted to do him proud, everybody checked their egos at the door. Nobody was out to grab any credit for themselves – there was a higher cause at play.'

From the runner who looked after Douglas's family on the Moorgate set, to the performer who was so desperate to be part of the production that he was willing to deal with the claustrophobia that he knew he would suffer by being inside the Vogon soldier suit, everyone connected to the movie of *The Hitchhikers Guide to the Galaxy* had a love for their work, and wanted to be there to be part of such a historic project.

'Someone said to me during filming that it must be tiring me out,' Joel Collins recalls. 'And I said that nothing could compare to the pain I went through during those early days, trying to come up with the ideas with Garth. Over the course of a few months it amazingly started to make sense, and look

like a film, but it all came from blood, guts and enthusiasm. For Nick, Garth and me, it was like being in a candy shop when we had 36 people in the art department churning away, with Frank Walsh from the old school, designing alongside Dan May using all the most up-to-date computer techniques. It was the chance of a lifetime to do something like this. The more the complications, the more we found it exciting. We put together a package of ideas that we nail-bitingly hoped would work but we never knew if they would actually do so.'

'It's been going on for so long,' producer Nick Goldsmith says, 'that everything seems to have moulded into one big pinnacle moment for me. We knew from the start that we'd really have to work hard. I discovered that when you make a film, you're not going to make it perfect. A film is made up of flaws, like life. When it works technically, you move onto the next piece. The production team were fantastic: in a way

it was quite difficult to let go a bit and let other people do their jobs, but Caroline Hewitt and Todd Arnow were fantastic as co-producers on the film.'

Garth Jennings recalls the surprise he felt when he saw the first rough-cut assembly of the film shortly after principal photography finished: 'It was two-and-a-half hours long, and it fell to pieces every two to three minutes,' the director says, pouring himself yet another cup of tea. 'But what I couldn't get over was that it was what we had set out to make. It was the movie we'd all gone to try and make work.'

Index

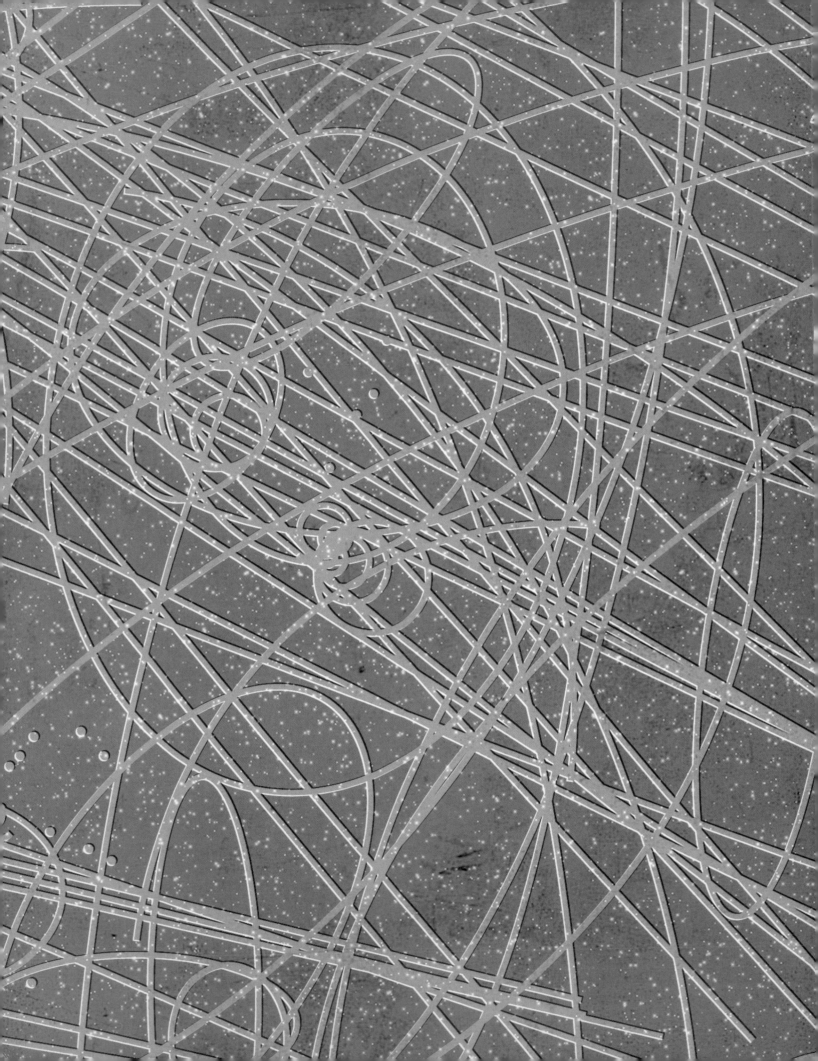